Working Effectively with Trustees:
Building Cooperative Campus Leadership

by Barbara E. Taylor

ASHE-ERIC Higher Education Report No. 2, 1987

Prepared by

Clearinghouse on Higher Education
The George Washington University

Published by

ASHE Association for the Study of
Higher Education

Jonathan D. Fife, Series Editor

Cite as
Taylor, Barbara E. *Working Effectively with Trustees: Building Cooperative Campus Leadership.* ASHE-ERIC Higher Education Report No. 2. Washington, D.C.: Association for the Study of Higher Education, 1987.

Managing Editor: Christopher Rigaux
Manuscript Editor: Barbara M. Fishel/Editech

The ERIC Clearinghouse on Higher Education invites individuals to submit proposals for writing monographs for the Higher Education Report series. Proposals must include:
1. A detailed manuscript proposal of not more than five pages.
2. A chapter-by-chapter outline.
3. A 75-word summary to be used by several review committees for the initial screening and rating of each proposal.
4. A vita.
5. A writing sample.

Library of Congress Catalog Card Number 87-71598
ISSN 0884-0040
ISBN 0-913317-38-1

Cover design by Michael David Brown, Rockville, Maryland

ERIC **Clearinghouse on Higher Education**
The George Washington University
One Dupont Circle, Suite 630
Washington, D.C. 20036-1183

ASHE **Association for the Study of Higher Education**
Texas A&M University
Department of Education Administration
Harrington Education Center
College Station, Texas 77843

Office of Educational
Research and Improvement
U.S. Department of Education

This publication was prepared partially with funding from the Office of Educational Research and Improvement, U.S. Department of Education, under contract no. 400-86-0017. The opinions expressed in this report do not necessarily reflect the positions or policies of OERI or the Department.

EXECUTIVE SUMMARY

The governance of colleges and universities by lay boards of
trustees is a ubiquitous feature of American higher education.
A relatively extensive literature describes the responsibilities
boards are advised to assume. Less attention is given to discussion of the activities boards actually undertake and the influence administrators and faculty members exercise over trustees'
performance. Nevertheless, we know that institutional personnel are critical determinants of a board's behavior and that
skillful management of the board can result in legitimation and
support for individual institutional personnel and for the college
or university itself. Therefore, administrators and faculty are
advised to understand the sources and nature of trustees' authority and by extension of their own influence on boards.

Why Are Institutions Governed by Lay Boards?
Through the late 19th century, institutions were controlled by
lay boards because the early colleges were seen as too crucial
to be left in the hands of faculties, which at the time were
young, undereducated, and limited in size. Boards controlled
by prominent clergy, government officials, and eventually by
businessmen provided resources and legitimation to fledgling
institutions and were responsible in large measure for ensuring
that colleges and universities responded to society's changing
needs.

   As faculty and administrative professionalism and institutional complexity have increased during the past century, however, many observers have suggested that lay governing boards
are anachronistic at best and that the ability of boards to govern
is so constrained as to make the system superfluous. Yet it continues—and has even been adopted by recently founded institutions. In part, the system has been so thoroughly
institutionalized in law and tradition that it cannot easily be
supplanted. But perhaps more important, alternatives to lay
trusteeship, such as control by the faculty or direct governance
by the state, are seen as even less desirable.

What Criticisms Are Leveled at Lay Boards and
What Defenses Are Offered?
Criticisms and defenses of lay trusteeship concern the nature of
the public interest in higher education, the contributions of
boards to serving that interest, the legitimacy of trustees, and
their competence to govern.

   In both independent and public institutions, boards are

viewed as a means of representing the broadly defined public interest in higher education by simultaneously shielding the institution from shortsighted external pressure and ensuring that parochial internal interests are not served at the expense of essential societal needs. Particularly in public institutions, however, boards have sometimes been criticized as little more than conduits for interference from outsiders who neither understand nor appreciate the academic enterprise.

The legitimacy of trustees has been challenged on grounds that boards are unrepresentative and incompetent to govern. Boards are seen as too socially and demographically homogeneous to govern diverse institutions and not conversant enough with academic matters to presume to substitute their judgment for that of academic experts within the institution. Contrary views hold that the relatively high social status of board members and their professional independence from the academic enterprise provide them with credibility, as they represent the institution to the society on which it depends for support. Moreover, because faculty are specialists, they are sometimes viewed as little more competent than trustees to make judgments about the institution as a whole and too often self-serving to place the long-term welfare of the institution ahead of their short-term personal and professional interests.

Finally, some who support lay trusteeship in concept criticize the performance of many boards. It has been argued, for example, that trustees have delegated too much authority, that they commit too little time to governance, and that they have abdicated responsibility for the central academic functions of their institutions. In other instances, however, boards have been credited with promoting higher education's interests to a sometimes skeptical public, raising needed resources, and serving as a stabilizing influence in periods of organizational change.

What Responsibilities Are Assigned to Boards and What Do They Actually Do?

Within the limitations specified by law and institutional charters, boards are assigned responsibility for all aspects of institutional management. The literature describes a broad and sometimes conflicting range of duties, including the obligation to perform or oversee all of the institution's major academic and administrative functions and to do so by means consistent with prevailing academic norms. Emphasis is placed on the board's responsibilities to promulgate overriding policies that will guide presidents and others in the day-to-day operation of institutions.

In fact, evidence suggests that boards are more likely to involve themselves in the operating details of colleges and universities than in broad policy making. It is often difficult to distinguish policy from administration and, given the range of policy matters to be decided, virtually impossible to assign all responsibility for policy making to trustees. The knowledge and experience of administrators, traditions of faculty authority over academic and allied matters, the board's operating style, and the realities of environmental dependence appear to influence the actual exercise of board authority. Moreover, trustees may in effect decline to govern by giving little time to their trusteeships and by dealing with less controversial matters to avoid conflict.

A board's increased activity appears to be associated with recovery from institutional financial crisis as well as with the achievement of significant quality gains in basically healthy colleges and universities. In the former case, the activity tends to be operational, while in the latter case, it is largely supportive of administrators and externally oriented.

How Can Administrators and Faculty Share
Authority with Trustees?
The notion that boards should share with others responsibility for crucial decisions and activities is a logical outgrowth of observations concerning the nature of authority in colleges and universities. "Formal authority is based on legitimacy. . .and position, whereas functional authority is based on competence and person" (Mortimer and McConnell 1978, p. 19). Trustees rely mainly on formal authority, while administrators and faculty members seeking to influence boards do so largely through the exercise of functional authority. In fact, boards share considerable authority with institutional constituents, including presidents, other administrators, and faculty members. Groups generally claim certain "spheres of influence" (Baldridge, Curtis, and Riley 1978, p. 71) that appear to correspond to tradition and expertise.

The effective relationship between board and president is frequently described as a harmonious partnership based on mutual support and trust. Yet the relationship is paradoxical. The board is vested with final authority over institutional policies and practices and is authorized to hire and dismiss the president. At the same time, the board depends on the president for information and for development and execution of policy. Thus, it is probably more accurate to describe the relationship between trustees and senior administrators as one of mutual dependence rather than partnership. Such "exchange relationships" exchange the board's formal authority for administrators' functional authority.

Boards cannot do their work without the assistance of others. Characteristically, this assistance includes the responsibilities to educate, inform, and motivate the board. In controlling these processes, administrators assume powerful positions vis-à-vis boards, which technically occupy a superior position. In fact, the president becomes the acknowledged leader of many boards whose members look to the chief executive for ideas, recommended actions, and information about the board's appropriate behavior. Thus, senior administrators can markedly influence a board's work by spending time communicating with trustees, controlling board agendas and background information, influencing the selection and development of trustees, motivating trustees' desired behavior, and establishing strong relationships with faculty and other constituents who legitimate administrative authority.

Faculty members' influence on boards derives from the desire of many administrators and trustees to share authority with faculty and from the fact that influence derives from functional as well as formal authority. Faculty willing to press for a voice in governance are frequently heeded, owing primarily to the political nature of much decision making in colleges and universities.

Faculty members may seek to influence boards in a variety of direct and indirect ways. They are advised first to persuade and then support the president and thus strengthen indirectly their own position in relation to the board. Faculty should also treat trustees as resources and allies, using trustees' talents and strengthening the board's ability to withstand threats from the environment.

ADVISORY BOARD

CONTENTS

FOREWORD

For higher education institutions, the board of trustees has two
distinctive characteristics. First, as lay people or non-education
specialists, they represent special interest groups concerned
with the welfare of the institution. Second, a board has the ultimate authority that allows others to participate in and contribute
expertise for the decision-making process. In short, all authority and power, including academic affairs, rests with the board
of trustees.

Over the years, the problems facing colleges and universities
have become so diverse and specialized that it is impossible for
any governing board to have in-depth knowledge of every area
they must cover. Therefore it is the wise board and the smart
president who seek the support of administrators and faculty at
all levels.

As most board members serve only on a part-time basis,
their time must be used as efficiently as possible. The president, in the role of gatekeeper, can both limit the board's be-
siegement from external superfluous information, and also
carefully guard against practices that isolate trustees from the
reality of the institution. This objective of having an informed
yet not overburdened board of trustees is critical to the effective functioning of the institution.

More than any other person on campus, the president is the
crucial player in developing an effective board. He or she must
be willing to share the responsibility of keeping the board informed. As gatekeeper, the president can influence how harmo-
niously information vital to an institution's missions and
objectives is shared. The president can also make sure that all
the players—administrators, faculty members, and trustees—
understand their roles in the governance structure. The more
clearly each role is understood, the more automatic information
sharing becomes.

This report by Barbara Taylor, the director of the Institute
for Trustee Leadership at the Association of Governing Boards
of Universities and Colleges, examines the authority and governance responsibility of boards of trustees and then reviews the
importance of providing information into the decision-making
process. She carefully articulates each area of responsibility for
the board of trustees, and then examines the factors affecting
the success or failure of a given board.

The relationship between a lay board of trustees and on-
campus academic and administrative personnel is unique to
higher education. Because the locus of control for board-institu-

tion relationships has been held by the president and, as a consequence, only a few other personnel have traditionally been involved, the relationship of trustees to all members of the institution has often been overlooked. This report fills that gap. This report should also encourage colleges and universities to develop a more open flow of communication among all levels.

Jonathan D. Fife
Series Editor
Professor and Director
ERIC Clearinghouse on Higher Education
The George Washington University

ACKNOWLEDGMENTS

I am grateful for helpful comments on an earlier draft of this report from Richard P. Chait, Richard T. Ingram, and Kenneth P. Mortimer.

INTRODUCTION

This report considers the characteristics and practices of governing boards of higher education institutions and systems and the means by which administrators and faculty can work more effectively with trustees.

To understand the nature of administrative and faculty influence on boards, one must first consider the sources of the American system of governance by lay persons, the responsibilities boards are assigned and undertake, the characteristics of the boards and trustees produced by the system, and the factors that motivate trustees' participation in governance. Thus, this report considers several issues and questions:

- *The history and evolution of lay trusteeship.* What conditions produced the singularly American system of governance of higher education by boards comprised of lay people? How has the system changed over time? Why has it survived?
- *Composition of the board and selection of trustees.* What are the characteristics of trustees, how are they selected, and what are the effects of these factors on a board's performance? What motivates individuals to join and participate on boards?
- *Areas of the board's responsibility.* What responsibilities are assigned to trustees? Which are considered most important and why?
- *Factors affecting the work of the board.* What responsibilities for governance do boards actually assume? What factors constrain trustees' ability to govern? Why do some boards appear to abdicate responsibility for governance? And what factors may cause them to become more active?
- *Board structures and processes.* How do a board's officers, committee system, agendas, and meetings affect the nature and quality of its work? How is a board's performance assessed?
- *Sharing authority with trustees.* How do the president, other administrators, and faculty interact with boards? What are the sources of their influence? What are the risks and rewards for senior administrators and faculty associated with direct contact with trustees? How can institutional personnel contribute to the board's improved performance and enhance their own relationships with their boards?

The Early Colleges

Much of the history of higher education in the United States can be understood by studying the roots and evolution of lay trusteeship, a mechanism of governance devised in Europe but never fully realized until modified in America to suit uniquely American conditions (Cowley 1980; Hofstadter and Metzger 1955).

Harvard College, founded in 1636 as America's first institution of higher education, was no less than a necessity to Puritans who intended to tame and civilize a new world. The Puritans' fundamental purposes could not be realized without "a learned clergy and a lettered people," which Harvard was established to provide (Morison 1935, p. 45). But the English system of extensive faculty self-governance with only negligible external influence could not be transplanted directly to the New World. The Massachusetts Bay Colony had neither the resources nor the scholars to duplicate an Oxford or a Cambridge, and it could not afford to wait for a faculty-controlled system of higher education to evolve (Rudolph 1962).

When the Massachusetts General Court passed an act providing for Harvard's creation, it also appointed 12 men—six government officials and six clergymen—to a Board of Overseers with authority to hire staff, manage finances, set academic standards, and otherwise tend to the college's affairs (Brubacher and Rudy 1968; Clark 1976; Rudolph 1962). Both Harvard and William and Mary, America's second college, later appointed institutional boards paralleling their lay boards in an effort to emulate the English model of governance with which they were most familiar. Neither institutional board had extensive powers, however. In the case of Harvard, the "corporation" eventually attained those powers but only after it had been taken over by outsiders. At William and Mary, the institutional board survived but with its limited authority even more severely curtailed. Control of Yale, America's third college, was given absolutely to a nonresident lay board, and it was the Yale model that set the American pattern (Brubacher and Rudy 1968; Hofstadter and Metzger 1955; Rudolph 1962).

One compelling explanation for the scarcity and failure of institutional boards was in the nature of the early professoriate. Until the latter half of the 19th century, few faculty members were much older or better educated than their students. A typical college might have a president who spent much of his time teaching and three or four "tutors," recent graduates waiting

Much of the history of higher education in the United States can be understood by studying the roots and evolution of lay trusteeship.

for appointments as ministers. It was not until well into the 18th century that Harvard or Yale had its first professor and not for many years after that until professors outnumbered tutors (Hofstadter and Metzger 1955, p. 124).

The president was often quite powerful in the early college, having been delegated much of the board's formal authority. The tutors, in contrast, rarely had any authority at all. They presided over students' recitations from an unchanging classical curriculum and spent much of the remainder of their time disciplining their students, most of whom were years younger than what is now considered college aged (Rudolph 1962).

19th Century Modifications
During the latter half of the 19th century, boards, presidents, and faculties changed under the influence of a growing, dynamic, and pragmatic American society. Americans were fascinated by science and technology and the wealth to be found through commerce and individual effort. The immutable classical curriculum, perceived as being of no practical use in such a society, began to collapse. Colleges that failed to offer "practical" subjects suffered in the competition for students, resources, and public support (Rudolph 1962).

Clerics, who had dominated governing boards for more than 200 years, began to be replaced by businessmen and alumni whose worldly ties meant prestige, philanthropy, and popular support for the colleges (Brubacher and Rudy 1968). Such boards were far less likely to hire the traditional clergyman-president associated with the moribund classical curriculum. Instead, a new kind of president—whether lawyer, businessman, politician, or scholar—who supported practical programs and was at home with worldly affairs, became the board's usual choice (Rudolph 1962; Veysey 1965).

Faculty who could teach practical subjects were crucial to the colleges' survival. At the extreme, such emerging institutions as Johns Hopkins, created to emulate the German research university, were highly faculty centered. At most colleges, however, faculty may have been increasingly important to institutional success, but their treatment at the hands of boards and presidents would not have so indicated. Presidents, as local agents of nonresident boards, had long since ceased acting as the first among equals typical of the rectors of English universities. Faculty views largely went unrepresented before most boards, whose opinions of the professoriate tended to be unflattering at best. Competition among institutions for students was intense in the late 19th century, and tuition was kept low by minimizing faculty salaries. Ironically, boards comprised of prominent businessmen tended to deprecate the value and contributions of faculty who would work for so little (Rudolph 1962). Thus, even while the importance of faculty was growing, their influence on the policies of most institutions remained limited until the present century.

To the businessman-trustee accustomed to bureaucracy and specialization, the organizational structure emerging in the larger institutions of the late 19th century probably seemed logical. The board presided at the head of the hierarchy; the president, and later his staff, attended to academic matters, budgets, public relations, and record keeping; the faculty exercised limited authority over curriculum and taught the classes; and students studied and were graduated (Rudolph 1962).

While retaining formal and near total authority over their institutions, however, few boards were dictatorial; presidents were far more likely to act as autocrats. This era witnessed the strong, institution-building president whose vision frequently outstripped that of the board and who as a result sometimes goaded recalcitrant trustees into sharing a broadened view of the institution and raising funds to support it. Daniel Coit Gilman, Johns Hopkins's founding president, for example, apparently cajoled his board into adopting advanced research as the institution's primary mission (Veysey 1965). Ambitious presidents in this and later periods often imposed their view of an increasingly complex enterprise on their perplexed, preoccupied, or geographically distant boards of trustees (Carnegie Commission 1973a; Veysey 1965).

Few enterprising presidents doubted the value of an influential board, however. Some institutions owed their existence to individual benefactors, and many others achieved respectability through their association with prominent citizens. In general, to attract money, students, and prestige, institutions had to conform in all basic respects to the established American structure, including the lay board (Veysey 1965). Thus, even state universities founded in the late 19th century and later adopted lay governance, which by that time had become ubiquitous and entrenched (Epstein 1974).

Perceiving the need for a new balance of power between lay and internal forces, A. Lawrence Lowell, president of Harvard in the early 20th century, argued that colleges needed both lay *and* institutional control. Without lay influence, the institution could lose touch with society. But without expert control from within, it would lose its intellectual authority. Similarly, Nicholas Murray Butler, president of Columbia University in the late 19th century, distinguished between policy formulation as the board's province and policy execution as an internal institutional matter (Brubacher and Rudy 1968).

Conflict between Boards and Faculties

Despite efforts to articulate appropriate roles for each academic constituency, conflict between boards and faculties continued to increase. Faculty were becoming more specialized, professional, and essential to the success of ever larger and more complex institutions. But trustees, accustomed to viewing faculty as employees, were reluctant to give them much heed. During the period between 1890 and 1920, boards and sometimes presidents made a number of well-publicized attempts to dismiss faculty members because of their intellectual or political views (Brubacher and Rudy 1968). It was the Progressive era, when reform movements assumed great importance, both providing faculty with issues to champion and fostering a social climate that encouraged free expression (Rudolph 1962).

Faculty members' discontent culminated in 1915 with the founding of the American Association of University Professors (AAUP), which articulated the professoriate's aspirations for shared authority in institutional decision making. Essentially, the AAUP's principles called for faculty to exercise primary responsibility for academic policy making and to share authority with trustees for the selection and dismissal of presidents and academic administrators. The AAUP also argued that to carry out these responsibilities, faculty members would require the protections of academic freedom and tenure (Brubacher and Rudy 1968).

While many boards initially resisted the professoriate's rise to power, the movement eventually became irresistible. Growth in institutional size and complexity and a concomitant emphasis on faculty expertise and specialization required governing boards to accept faculty as a potent institutional force (Veysey 1965). The rise of academic departments and faculty governance structures helped institutionalize faculty authority, leading one observer to conclude that "the history of university organization in the 20th century has been an account of the disintegration of the traditional form of government" in which

trustees exercise formal authority through a president who
serves as chief executive officer (Duryea 1973, p. 36).

Criticisms and Defenses of Contemporary Lay Trusteeship
Despite predictions of the decline or demise of lay trusteeship,
it remains a near ubiquitous but still controversial feature of
American higher education. Common themes found in the discussion of contemporary trusteeship include the nature of the
public interest in higher education, the contributions of boards
to serving that interest, the legitimacy of trustees, and their
competence to govern.

Boards and the public interest in higher education
From the founding of the earliest American colleges, the public
interest in higher education has been personified in both independent and public institutions by the lay board of trustees. A
common defense of boards is that they protect the broadly defined public interest by simultaneously shielding the institution
from shortsighted external interference and ensuring that parochial internal interests are not served at the expense of essential
societal needs.

Even universities founded in England during the past 200
years adopted structures of governance more reminiscent of the
American pattern than of the Oxford/Cambridge model. They
began as teaching institutions sponsored by lay people who
hired faculty and admitted students, and, as in the early American colleges, the founders of these English institutions sought
to protect the public interest by appointing governing boards
dominated by lay people (Cowley 1980; McConnell 1971).

Boards of independent institutions assume a trust that binds
them to a long-term perspective on the institution's purposes,
social responsibilities, and vitality. Even public institutions, at
least in principle, are not responsible to the immediate public
will as legislators and governors are (Epstein 1974). The adoption in American public institutions of the trustee model has
served to protect universities from the politicization commonly
seen in other countries whose universities are operated as agencies of the state (Zwingle 1980b). Therefore, given that some
form of public control is inevitable, it is said that knowledgeable people will always prefer the trustee system to direct governance by the state (Epstein 1974).

Some view the board of a public institution as little more
than "a conduit for political interference," however (Galbraith

1967, p. 34). Indeed, some state officials resent boards that identify themselves more with their institutions than with the immediate interests of the state (Epstein 1974).

Legitimacy and competence to govern
The legitimacy of trustees is often challenged on the grounds that the oligarchical character of governing boards is inconsistent with democratic ideals (Epstein 1974; Hodgkinson 1971; Kramer 1965). Boards are seen as unrepresentative: too often old, wealthy, white, and male to govern diverse institutions (Gould 1973; Zwingle 1985).

Some critics charge that faculty should, and in fact do, control colleges and universities. Trustees are seen as outsiders who do not understand the academic enterprise and are incapable of governing it (Corson 1975; Epstein 1974; Zwingle 1985). Faculty in the "mature university" control the central business of the institution: appointments, curricula, and the conduct of research, rendering the lay governing board "an anachronism" (Galbraith 1967, p. 34). More recently, however, faculty influence in most institutions has been curtailed by a weakened job market, decreasing research funds, and pressure from external groups for greater authority (Baldridge, Curtis, and Riley 1978).

The view of trustees as incompetent to govern is based largely on the observation that few are professional educators. Two contrary views of competence hold that trustees' worldly knowledge is as valuable and necessary to the institution as the academic expertise of faculty members and that the competence of faculty to govern is exaggerated.

Most trustees have been exposed to other types of organizations whose management and educational methods may be instructive to higher education (Bean 1975). Trustees' external perspectives can provide their institutions with a more sophisticated understanding of environmental threats and opportunities (Dorsey 1980; Nelson 1980). With respect to faculty competence, it is said that faculty are specialists who frequently understand less than trustees do about the institution or the higher education enterprise as a whole (Corson 1973a; Martin 1974).

Even if faculty and administrators were deemed competent to govern, it is argued that any organization left entirely in charge of its own affairs will become self-serving, resistant to change, and increasingly remote from the public interest (Newman 1986; Pray 1975). "A collection of special advocates cannot be

expected to be a repository and a voice of judicial wisdom"
(Ruml and Morrison 1959, p. 7). Thus, if the operations of a
college or university were left entirely in the hands of faculty
and administrators, the institution would likely cease to function responsibly and effectively (Greenleaf 1974; Martin 1974).

In any case, expertise may not be the issue. Current conditions in American higher education promote the centralization
of authority in the hands of administrators and boards. Competition for resources and students within and among institutions
often necessitates high-level decisions concerning the allocation
of funds and the adoption of competitive strategies for the institution. And to the extent that authority moves to external
groups, the board's role as interpreter and protector of the institution increases (Carnegie Commission 1973a; Carnegie Foundation 1982; Corson 1970; Ingram 1980b; Zwingle and
Mayville 1974).

The significance that continues to be accorded to the lay
governing board is illustrated in the founding of Hampshire
College in 1965. Hampshire was planned by a committee that
included no trustees from any of the four institutions sponsoring the new college, and almost no attention was given in the
planning documents prepared by the committee to the role, if
any, a governing board might play in the life of the institution
(Bean 1975). The college's first board was comprised of the
presidents of the sponsoring institutions, one former president,
and the college's primary benefactor. When Hampshire opened
in 1970, however, the board had expanded to 13 members and
included several nonacademics. As of 1987, it had 23 members
and its composition was typical of that found in comparable institutions. According to a college official, Hampshire, like
other American institutions, needed a lay board to provide it
with credibility and to enable it to attract public support.*

Performance of the board
Some who support the concept of lay trusteeship are critical of
the performance of many boards. Trustees have delegated too
much authority and merely serve to "satisfy the legal requirement [that a board exist] . . . and provide the cover of legitimacy" (Greenleaf 1974, p. 12). Too often they commit too
little time to governing, rubber stamp the recommendations of

*Peter Glucker 1987, personal communication.

others, and, in particular, abdicate responsibility for the central academic functions of their institutions (Corson 1973a; Gould 1973).

If trustees fail to govern, the failure may be endemic to the nature of contemporary institutions of higher education. Some see the lay governance system as becoming increasingly ceremonial, because boards of modern institutions cannot hope to exercise the complete authority assigned to them by statutes and charters (Corson 1975; Zwingle 1985).

Nevertheless, because of their informed and committed but detached perspective, trustees are credited with broadening access to higher education, choosing strong leadership, promoting academic freedom to a sometimes skeptical public, encouraging faculty concern for the whole institution rather than just its specialized parts, and raising the resources required for growth and development (Clark 1976; Greenleaf 1974; McGrath 1971; Newman 1973). At the same time, the lay board is seen as a stabilizing influence that discourages shortsighted change in response to short-lived public or institutional whims (Zwingle 1985). A recent study of 20 campuses judged as moving toward significantly increased academic excellence revealed that supportive boards of trustees were all but essential to the achievement of institutional excellence. Such boards promote unity within the institution and deal effectively with powerful external constituents (Gilley, Fulmer, and Reithlingshoefer 1986, p. 12).

Given the catalog of defenses and criticisms, it is not surprising to see trusteeship justified in terms reminiscent of Churchill: "It is the poorest form of government, except for all the others" (Cheit 1971, p. 5; see also Clark 1976). The board is essential, in part, by default:

> *No other mechanism can provide for governance so well, not the state, not the faculty, not the students, and not the faculty and students together. State control, as seen in many nations, tends to become both too bureaucratic and too representative of what society wants; the faculty is not generally chosen for its administrative talents and is divided administratively by its own special interests; the students are inexperienced and transient; and the students and the faculty are in certain significant disagreements about influence over academic matters* (Carnegie Commission 1973a, p. 32).

Composition of the Board
Demographics
College and university boards are described as "monolithic" in character: "white, Anglo-Saxon, Protestant, male, well-to-do business and professional men, over 50 in age" (Nason 1982, p. 55). Three studies undertaken over a 17-year period demonstrate the general accuracy of popular perceptions of composition but also underscore some slight shifts over time (Association of Governing Boards 1986; Gomberg and Atelsek 1977; Hartnett 1969).

- Representation of women and minorities on boards has increased, but not dramatically. In particular, the presence of black members on boards has remained steady at 6 percent since 1977.
- Women, minorities, and younger members are found more frequently on public than on independent boards and more often on single-campus than on multicampus boards.
- Business and professional people dominated board membership to as great an extent in 1985 as they did in 1968. These groups are more likely to be represented on independent than on public boards (see table 1).

Composition, size, and trustees' roles
The size and composition of boards can be explained in part by considering the roles trustees assume. Traditionally, "the choice of college trustees tended to follow the same pattern as financial support. The college whose special mission was defined by geography or religion usually drew all its trustees from within its particular parish, at least initially" (Jencks and Riesman 1968, p. 5).

As noted earlier, boards dominated by clergy before the Civil War came to be dominated by businessmen in the late 19th century as commerce and worldly affairs assumed greater importance in American society. Business trustees were able to attract the public support that produced funds and other resources for their institutions, and in many cases these board members were themselves important sources of funds.

It continues to be true today that institutions often use the composition of the board as a means of attracting needed environmental support in the form of funds, legitimation, or other crucial resources (Aldrich 1979; Middleton 1983; Pfeffer and Salancik 1978). A 1973 study of hospital boards may be in-

Institutions often use the composition of the board as a means of attracting needed environmental support in the form of funds, legitimation, or other crucial resources.

TABLE 1

CHANGES IN CHARACTERISTICS OF GOVERNING BOARD MEMBERS, 1968 TO 1985

(in percentages)

	1968[a]	1977[b]	1985[c]
Sex			
Male	86	85	80
Female	13	15	20
Race			
White	96	93	90
Black	1	6	6
Hispanic	NA	NA	1
Other minority	0	1	3
Unknown	3	0	0
Age			
35 or under	5	10	9
40–49	21	24	21
50–59	37	35	38
60–69	27	25	24
70 or over	9	7	8
Occupation[d]			
Business	36	34	37
Education	13	14	11
Professional service	15	13	14
Other (including retired)	34	38	38
Unknown	2	0	0

[a]Hartnett 1969.
[b]Gomberg and Atelsek 1977.
[c]Association of Governing Boards 1986.
[d]Occupational categories used in the Gomberg and Atelsek and the Association of Governing Boards studies are not strictly comparable. In the 1977 study, foundation executives were included in the business category, but in the 1985 study, they were counted in the "other" group. Social workers and accountants, included in "other" in 1977, were counted in the professional service category in 1985. Clergy, included in the professional service category in 1977, were counted among the "other" group in 1985.

structive in this regard. Nonprofit hospitals that depended primarily on local resources tended to have large boards comprised of local business leaders who concentrated on acquiring resources for their hospitals. In contrast, business people were not predominant on the boards of religious hospitals, whose resources came primarily from outside the community, and rather than concentrating on the acquisition of resources, those boards tended more to administrative matters (Pfeffer 1973).

Boards of higher education are often advised to seek diverse professional skills among their members. One observer goes so far as to call for a board that has among its members "a distinguished expert in the field of each commonly met problem": finance; theory of management and organization; higher education; plant management; public relations and development; alumni affairs; business, corporate, and social relations; labor; and politics (Pray 1975, pp. 9–10). Others write of the need for diverse operating styles and personal qualities among board members to provide a proper balance, for example, between activity and restraint (Zwingle 1985).

In each case, boards are using or being advised to seek trustees who can help the institution manage its environmental dependencies. A trustee with funds or access to them, with social status, political connections, professional skills useful for dealing with the environment, or personal qualities that enhance the board's functioning or legitimacy, the reasoning goes, can be a valuable asset.

One might conclude, then, that the underrepresentation of women and minorities, particularly on independent boards, reflects the perception that these individuals do not control sources of critical support. The slightly greater presence of women and minorities on public boards may reflect both public institutions' lesser reliance on private funds and a greater need for other, nonfinancial forms of support that depend in part on the perception that the board is representative.

The composition of a board can doubtless also be explained in part by the observation that nominees for board positions resemble those making the nominations (Duke University 1970). Whether trustees of a self-perpetuating board who select their own new members or government officials who appoint most public trustees, the nominators tend to be white, male, older, affluent, and business connected. And such individuals are likely to select people they know and are comfortable with— people like themselves.

Some observers have called for faculty membership on boards of their own institutions, a demand heard particularly often during the campus upheavals of the 1960s (McConnell

1971; McGrath 1971). Others have countered that such membership violates the principle that trustees are responsible to the public as a whole rather than to an individual constituency (Zwingle 1985). Moreover, because faculty trustees could not be expected to deal objectively with conditions of their employment, an inherent and intolerable conflict of interest would exist (Rauh 1973). To ensure an academic perspective on boards without risking conflict of interest, it has been suggested that boards include members who are academics from other institutions (Carnegie Commission 1973a; Martin 1974).

In fact, few boards include faculty from either their own or other institutions. Fewer than 1 percent of board members are faculty from the institution where they serve as trustees, and just 1.2 percent are faculty from other colleges or universities (Taylor 1987). It may well be that beyond arguments about conflict of interest, faculty are not found commonly on boards because they neither resemble the nominators nor are for the most part seen as useful in attracting support. Board consultation with faculty, which probably is important to establishing the board's internal legitimacy, can be accomplished in other ways (discussed later).

The size of a board may also be understood, at least in part, by environmental dependence. The more heterogeneous the institution's environment, the larger its board is likely to be (Pfeffer and Salancik 1978). Independent institutions, whose sources of funds are more diverse, would be expected to have larger boards with more ties to significant external sources of support. In contrast, public institutions, whose support comes largely from government sources, have a less diverse environment to manage and should consequently require a smaller board. In fact, independent boards, on average, have 32 members, while the mean for public boards is 11 trustees (Taylor 1987).

It may be misleading for two reasons, however, to assume a strict causal relationship between a board's size and the diversity of its environmental dependence. First, the size of public boards is set by statute rather than by the board itself. Left to decide for itself, a public board might well increase its membership. Second, many public institutions have created structures supplementary to the board to help manage their environments, including committees to advise the institution's administrative offices or academic programs, which are found more commonly in public than in independent institutions (Taylor 1987), and separately incorporated foundations charged with fund raising for public colleges and universities (Radock and Jacobson 1980).

Motivation to join the board

A corollary to the discussion of what institutions seek from board members is the issue of what motivates individuals to join boards. Most appear to be attracted for reasons of social status associated with trusteeship, the desire to provide public service, the opportunity to strengthen ties with other board members and affiliates of the institution, and the sense of loyalty many alumni feel for their alma maters (Auerbach 1961; Corson 1973b; Middleton 1983).

Individuals of higher status are most likely to accept memberships on the boards of organizations that are particularly significant in the community and that serve central social goals (Middleton 1983; Zald 1967). Those institutions seen as less significant are likely to have boards of comparably lower status. These second-tier boards, however, are likely to be minor league versions of the higher-status boards, including ''the 'right people'—politically, economically, and sometimes socially'' (Lee and Bowen 1971, p. 134).

Related to the desire to enhance personal prestige is the wish for affiliation with others that is also served by membership on a board. Trustees interact with government officials, civic and corporate leaders, and others both on and off the board who can provide valuable professional and social contacts (Middleton 1983).

The desire to provide public service is often seen as a prime motivator for trustees, one that is not inconsistent with the quest for personal social status (Auerbach 1961; Zwingle 1985). Once a member of the board, a trustee's enthusiasm for staying on it appears to relate to the perception that he or she is participating in important decisions and is making a difference in the performance of the institution. This motivation seems more decisive than the institution's goals in encouraging continuing involvement by trustees (Auerbach 1961; Corson 1973b).

Alumni appear particularly motivated to serve as trustees of their institutions. Nationally, 13 percent of public trustees and 31 percent of independent board members are alumni of the institutions they serve (Association of Governing Boards 1986, pp. 20–21). Trustees in one study of small, independent, liberal arts colleges reported that their boards' best members are alumni because they show a particularly deep interest in and loyalty to their institutions (Wood 1985). Perhaps it is for this reason that a study of recovery from financial stress in independent institutions reported anecdotally on the salutary effects of adding alumni to the board (Chaffee 1984). Some presidents sound a cautionary note, however, believing that "unbridled alumni influence results in a board [that] is parochial" (Wood 1985, p. 83).

Effects of composition on the board's functioning

Composition affects in a variety of ways the internal functioning of boards and their relations with their institutions. Boards dominated by trustees from the corporate and legal communities, for example, are thought to be interested in financial matters and the physical plant to a greater extent than the more broadly based board that is willing to venture into educational issues (Rauh 1973).

An alternative explanation for this observation considers the relative status of two "pure types" of boards: the homogeneous, conflict-averse board and the more broadly representative, constituent-oriented board (Middleton 1983).

The conflict-averse board reinforces the formal hierarchy of the institution and avoids interfering in administration. In fact, such boards may interact only with top management and so may not know enough about the institution as a whole to participate in its operations. The constituent-oriented board, in contrast, is likely to be a more heterogeneous group than that found in the conflict-averse board and is apt to represent the interests of various external groups rather than consider itself responsible for supporting the institution's administration. As a result, such boards may become involved in a wide variety of operational matters, at varying levels of specificity.

Conflict-averse boards, then, may limit their attention to "safe" issues like finances and the physical plant to minimize conflict, to avoid interfering in administration, and thus to reinforce the institution's formal hierarchy of authority. In contrast, constituent-oriented boards, accountable to multiple external groups and often in internal conflict, involve themselves more widely in institutional affairs to promote their individual agendas.

Within boards, the relative power of individual trustees varies with their control of needed external resources and their knowledge about internal operations of the institution (Zald

1969). Thus, the trustee of a constituent-oriented board who has ties to a crucial constituent group in the community, the board member who is a skilled investor and serves on a board whose staff has no comparable expertise, and the wealthy trustee who gives more than any other contributor to the institution's annual fund are powerful relative to other board members and are likely to be heeded by administrators and other trustees alike.

The influence of the powerful trustee may be countered by administrators who encourage the board to consider managerial details rather than broad policy matters (Kramer 1965). Moreover, the powerful trustee on a high-status board may be as averse to conflict as any other trustee and as committed to reinforcing the hierarchy of authority.

The attitudes of board members appear to be related to their occupational group, and in turn they influence faculty members' perceptions of the campus climate. Politically conservative trustees from business backgrounds tend also to be more conservative with respect to academic freedom and participatory governance on campus, and in fact faculty on such campuses perceive their environments as conservative. Women, blacks, and younger members on boards tend to be more liberal than their older, white, male counterparts and thus tend to be associated with institutions whose faculty perceive a more liberal campus environment (Hartnett 1970).

Selection of Trustees
Processes for selecting trustees vary greatly between the public and independent sectors of higher education. Most public trustees are popularly elected or appointed by governors or legislative bodies (see table 2). Popular election is considerably more prevalent among two-year institutions, while trustees are more likely to be appointed at four-year single- and multicampus institutions. Most trustees of independent institutions are selected by the board itself (self-perpetuation) or by constituent groups, such as alumni or sponsoring churches.

Despite differences in methods of selection, the result in both sectors is said to be boards that are demographically unrepresentative, uninformed about higher education, and, especially in public institutions, too often uncommitted to their institutions (Bean 1975; Besse 1973; Corson 1975; Lee and Bowen 1971; Nelson 1973).

TABLE 2
SELECTION OF TRUSTEES ACCORDING TO METHOD
(in percentages)

	Public Institutions				Independent Institutions		
	All	2-Year	4-Year Single Campus	4-Year Multi-campus	All	2-Year	4-Year
Self-perpetuation	2	1	2	0	61	61	61
Popular election	14	37	4	8	0	0	0
Appointment or election by governor or legislature	66	40	77	79	1	0	1
Election or appointment by constituent groups, such as alumni or church bodies	9	8	9	13	15	24	15
Combination of self-perpetuation and appointment by constituents	5	1	9	0	28	12	29
Other, including appointment by local governing bodies	19	23	18	16	5	6	5

Note: Columns may sum to more than 100 because of multiple responses to the same question.
Source: Taylor 1987.

Selection of trustees in public institutions

Disagreements over selection in public institutions concern the nature and effect on the selection process of inappropriate political influence (Kohn and Mortimer 1983). Elected boards are said to attempt to represent the people who voted them into office. Indeed, particularly when trustees are elected in local rather than in statewide elections, board members are often exposed to direct community pressure. As a result, many such boards tend to involve themselves in managerial detail in an effort to be responsible to constituents and—not incidentally—to be reelected (Brown and Walworth 1985–86; Gould 1973; Kerr and Gade 1986; Pray 1975; Zwingle 1980b). Some also think it questionable that many with the capacity to become effective trustees will subject themselves to the rigors and expense of campaigning for office (Kohn and Mortimer 1983).

Those who defend direct election of trustees claim that the process is more open and therefore more democratic than political appointment and that elected trustees have the independence needed to protect their institutions from governmental intrusion (Kohn and Mortimer 1983).

Critics of political appointment contend that politicians cannot ignore partisan considerations in selecting board members. As a result, appointed trustees may be unqualified, uninterested in serving the institution, and subject to partisan political pressure (Gould 1973; Kohn and Mortimer 1983; Lee and Bowen 1971; Pray 1975). The activities of such boards are likely to be influenced more by political than by substantive considerations (Newman 1973).

Some suggest that the political access available to appointed trustees is an advantage to public institutions dependent for support on governors or legislators. But because trustees' terms of office are not usually coterminus with those of the appointing person or body, many board members may be associated with previous rather than present office holders (Epstein 1974). A by-product of this arrangement is its contribution to greater board independence than otherwise might result from a political appointment process. Overlapping terms of office can produce a relationship between trustees and the appointing agency that has been likened to the connection between Supreme Court justices and the president of the United States; short of attempts to change the rules of appointment and tenure, the governor or legislature must wait for vacancies to occur before politically desirable appointments can be made (Epstein 1974).

How then can the selection process for public boards be improved? Most suggestions involve the nominating and screening of candidates for board membership by panels comprised of educators, civic groups, alumni, students, business and professional groups, civic associations, political parties, and so on (Carnegie Commission 1973a; Corson 1975; Lee and Bowen 1971; Nason 1982; National Commission 1980b; Rauh 1969). Such a committee could be charged with assessing requirements for board membership for demographic balance and range of competencies, searching for and screening candidates, consulting with incumbent trustees and the chief executive, and nominating members to the appointing agency. Where trustees are elected, the committee could nominate the candidates or, at a minimum, publicly endorse their preferred choices (Nason 1982; National Commission 1980b).

Some doubt whether such screening devices are wise or workable. A nominating group that includes enough educators to legitimate it in the eyes of the institution "endangers the essence of trusteeship as traditionally understood—that citizens representing the public should govern the university in behalf of the state to which it belongs" (Epstein 1974, pp. 89–90). As to workability, it seems doubtful to at least one observer that very many governors, legislators, or electing publics would voluntarily restrict their freedom to select the trustees they favor, even if they retain the right to choose from among a group of nominees (Epstein 1974).

Variations in the quality of boards among states, within states, and over time appear attributable to the traditions that adhere to appointment processes (Education Commission of the States 1986). When those responsible for selecting trustees consider candidates' commitment and interest as well as their politics, better boards are likely to result, and a tradition of effective boards begets boards of high quality.

Selection of trustees in independent institutions

The most common criticism leveled at selection processes of trustees in independent institutions is that they are "at worst haphazard and at best casual" (National Commission 1980a, p. 6; see also Besse 1973; Zwingle 1985). As one board member describes the selection process in the nonprofit sector generally, "Most . . . boards sort of stumble into adding people. They say, 'There's somebody good' and put them on the board. . . .

We must know why we are actually putting people there" (Mahoney 1985, p. 11).

Self-perpetuation tends above all to encourage the appointment of new board members who will "fit in" and to weed out those who are "deviant" (Middleton 1983, p. 26; see also Kramer 1965). In addition to serving that goal, boards that select new members purposively may be thought of doing so as a means of managing their environment. As suggested earlier, representatives of significant external groups are coopted by the institution as a strategy for obtaining resources, exchanging information, creating interinstitutional commitments, and establishing legitimacy with those outside the institution (Pfeffer and Salancik 1978, p. 161).

As a first step toward assembling a board that meets the needs of a particular institution, a board profile can be developed that describes the demographic composition and range of skills characterizing the current board. This exercise demonstrates where the board is strong or deficient and as vacancies arise provides guidance for assessing the suitability of prospective new members (Gale 1984).

The board is advised to have a nominating or membership committee charged with continuously searching for prospective trustees, assessing their qualifications in light of the board's needs, identifying the requirements for a given appointment to the board, and recommending candidates to the board to fill vacancies (Nason 1982; National Commission 1980a).

Recruiting new trustees can be difficult for all but the most prestigious institutions. Virtually all boards want influential, wealthy trustees who have an abiding interest in the institution, but few colleges have large numbers of such people among their alumni, usually the primary source of talent for independent institutions (Wood 1985). Institutions are therefore advised to seek out as prospective trustees people who are rising rapidly in their careers and are willing to work. Such people, who are "committed to the institution before they reach the top, become investments in the future" (Gale 1984, p. 9; see also National Commission 1980a).

Cultivating prospective trustees calls for making the effort to familiarize the individual with the institution and to pique his or her interest with invitations to the campus and to social events, such as dinner with current trustees and the president (Gale 1984).

The invitation to the prospective board member should be made in person by the president and at least one trustee, probably the chair. It should include a specific description of a trustee's responsibilities and an explanation of the reasons that particular person is being asked to join the board (Gale 1984; National Commission 1980a; O'Connell 1985).

Trustees' terms of office

Trustees' terms are longer on average in the public than the independent sector and are less likely to be subject to limitations on reappointment (see table 3).

The selection process for trustees of public institutions doubtless limits renewals sufficiently so that fewer formal regulations are required. Turnover among governors and legislators and shifting attitudes among the electing public probably ensure that board membership also will change over time. In fact, the somewhat longer terms of public trustees are probably crucial to forestalling excessive turnover and undue partisanship within the board's membership. Long, staggered terms usually prevent a single governor or legislature from packing a board with trustees of a particular political persuasion or the voting public from selecting an entire board in one election (Epstein 1974).

The issue of turnover in the independent sector is more problematic because, barring a trustee's resignation or formal limitations on reappointment, in most cases it is the board itself that must be willing to deny reappointment, a discomfiting prospect for conflict-averse boards comprised of people chosen in large measure because they "fit in." Yet the possibility of lifetime membership can make it difficult to rid the board of underperforming trustees (Gale 1984; National Commission 1980a; Wood 1985).

Most boards resist imposing a limit on length of term or a mandatory retirement age because such practices ensure that the best trustees as well as the least effective ones will be cycled off the board. And even if the hiatus is temporary, the individual may lose interest in the intervening time or be "pirated" by another board (Gale 1984, p. 14). Moreover, a replacement will have to be found, which, given the difficulties associated with recruiting new trustees, is a prospect many boards wish to avoid.

To ensure turnover that does not result in the complete severing of trustees' ties to the board, many boards confer honorary or emeritus status on valued trustees who have exceeded man-

TABLE 3
TRUSTEES' TERMS OF OFFICE AND LIMITATIONS ON REAPPOINTMENT

	Public Institutions				Independent Institutions		
	All	*2-Year*	*4-Year Single Campus*	*4-Year Multi-campus*	*All*	*2-Year*	*4-Year*
Mean length of term (years)	6	5	6	6	4	4	4
Percent of institutions that limit number of trustees terms	24	10	31	26	42	46	42
Mean maximum number of terms allowed (where limits exist)	2	2	2	2	3	3	3
Percent of institutions that allow reappointment/reelection after a waiting period	45	29	49	44	7	17	7
Mean length of waiting period (where waiting period exist)	2	1	2	2	1	1	1
Percent of institutions with a mandatory retirement age for trustees	3	1	3	3	23	16	24
Mean mandatory retirement age	71	75	70	70	71	72	71

Source: Taylor 1987.

datory retirement age or reached the board's limit on length of term. Honorary trustees usually may serve as members of board committees and may participate without vote in board meetings. Boards of independent institutions have an average of four honorary trustees each (Taylor 1987).

Techniques for ridding the board of ineffective members include assigning the nominating committee responsibility for evaluating trustees' performance and expecting the chair to ask underperforming trustees to step down (Gale 1984; National Commission 1980a).

Summary

Most boards are comprised predominantly of white, male businessmen and professionals. Board composition has changed little in recent years, primarily because of the need of colleges and universities to attract environmental support and legitimation to which many such trustees have access. Moreover, the selection processes tend to produce homogeneous, conflict-averse boards comprised of people who will "fit in." An exception is the constituent-oriented board, many of which are popularly elected.

Individuals are motivated to join boards for reasons of social prestige, desire to provide public service, access to powerful persons, and/or loyalty to the institution.

AREAS OF THE BOARD'S RESPONSIBILITY

A larger body of literature describes in both substance and process what boards should do than what they actually do (Brown 1986). Most of these lists of responsibilities center around policy making, financing the institution, staffing, and interpreting the institution to its environment (Kramer 1981; Middleton 1983), and the responsibilities mentioned most consistently can be summarized as follows:

1. Maintain the trust
2. Delegate authority
3. Raise and steward funds
4. Approve the budget
5. Develop and preserve physical facilities
6. Oversee academic affairs
7. Appoint, support, and evaluate the president
8. Arbitrate internal disputes
9. Establish goals and evaluate progress
10. Act as bridge and buffer to the environment
11. Stimulate change
12. Act responsibly.

Trustees are held legally responsible for their actions, and experts predict that the future will bring even more legal exposure to governing boards.

Maintain the Trust

Boards exist to provide continuity, stability, and integrity to protect the institution's mission, ''to make certain that long-term values are not sacrificed for short-term gains'' (Nason 1982, pp. 19–20). Fulfilling this responsibility requires that trustees concern themselves with the institution's activities as well as with its property (Zwingle 1985) and, indeed, that board members accept responsibility for all of the major decisions that influence the institution's quality and character (Corson 1973a). Thus, trustees must be knowledgeable about the institution and about governance (Fisher 1969), they must be committed to higher education and to the goals of the institution (Cheit 1971), and they must seek expert guidance from the president and faculty (Zwingle 1985).

Maintaining the trust is more than a purely ethical matter. Trustees are held legally responsible for their actions, and experts predict that the future will bring even more legal exposure to governing boards (Association of Governing Boards 1985; Ingram 1980b). Potential areas of concern include failure to review management, evaluate policies, and respond appropriately to financial crises (Pray 1974).

Courts expect that boards will know and abide by the law,

disclose and avoid participating in matters where their interests conflict with those of the institution, and act in good faith to protect the institution's integrity (Lascell and Hallenbeck 1980; Weeks 1980; Woodruff 1976).

Delegate Authority

Despite their legal authority, trustees are a legislative and not an executive body, and "execution of policy must be scrupulously left in the hands of the president" (Fisher 1969, p. 8). Indeed, one observer goes so far as to declare, "No argument or principle comes to mind [that] would entitle a board of trustees to act as the final or supreme authority in all the important affairs of the university—legal provisions in the board's charter notwithstanding" (Mason 1972, p. 27). In fact, in such areas as fund raising and hiring a president, trustees are often very much involved in the execution of policy. Moreover, few observers agree that boards should relinquish final authority for all other important institutional policy matters.

Trustees are encouraged to delegate authority for two reasons. First, the professional expertise of the faculty and administration renders them more competent than the board to make and execute many institutional decisions, or at least to collaborate with the board in doing so (Corson 1980; Mortimer and McConnell 1978). Second, absentee trustees have neither the time nor the information to carry out all of the responsibilities legally assigned to them. This situation could be remedied by making chairmanship of the board a full-time position and assigning the board a staff of its own (Greenleaf 1974), but such suggestions have never found wide support.

Trustees are told they can delegate authority but not responsibility (Corson 1977), and so devices for helping trustees "keep their noses in" and "their fingers out" are offered (Corson 1975, p. 268). Most emphasize the value of boards' asking questions of administrators as a means of monitoring the institution's functioning (Corson 1973a; Wood 1984b). Moreover, trustees are told that their concern should be with ensuring that the institution is well run rather than with running it (Carnegie Commission 1973a; Corson 1980).

Raise and Steward Funds

Lists of trustees' responsibilities are virtually unanimous in including fund raising and investment as key duties. They are seen as the primary manifestation of the board's responsibility to maintain the trust, and perhaps as important, trustees are viewed as more capable than most institutional personnel of raising and investing money. "No one, not even the president, is in as good a position to ask for support as the trustees, whose position gives them a special perspective, who are clearly not self-seeking, and whose commitment to the institution is seen as testimony to its worth" (Nason 1982, p. 27).

Similarly, boards are assumed to have capable investors among their members (or are encouraged to appoint such trustees), and, in fact, one recent study found that "sharply focused trustee involvement in the investment process resulted in improved [endowment] performance" (Academy for Educational Development 1985, p. 3).

Writers on trusteeship encourage far more direct involvement by board members in fund raising and investment than in most other areas of responsibility. A former college president and authority on fund raising argues unambiguously that successful fund raising requires that trustees be "exploited" and that they be "deeply involved" in all aspects of the program. "No fund raising program achieves success without strong board leadership" (Fisher 1984, p. 165).

Similarly, trustees are told they have a responsibility to "manage" the endowment and any temporary fund balances on hand (Nason 1982, p. 29; see also Academy for Educational Development 1985). It is significant that, unlike many other responsibilities, trustees are not told in this case that they have merely the duty to oversee the management of fund raising and investment.

The board's responsibility for fund raising is traditionally assumed to include personal giving and solicitation by trustees, particularly trustees of independent institutions (Bean 1975; Fisher 1984; Kinnison 1984; O'Connell 1985; Radock 1983; Radock and Jacobson 1980). Increasingly, the more recent literature treats the role of boards of public institutions in obtaining resources and considers the role in public policy of trustees of independent institutions in situations where state and federal policies affect support for independent institutions or for their students. Consequently, trustees are encouraged to engage in lobbying at the state and federal levels (Nason 1982) and in general to broaden their concern for the institution's activities involving government relations (Radock and Jacobson 1980).

Approve the Budget

Stated simply, trustees are advised that they are responsible for seeing "that the bills are paid" (Nason 1982, p. 24). This responsibility is viewed as a fundamental aspect of the board's role as preserver of the trust, and as such its significance is considered to extend well beyond the literal obligation to ensure that this month's electric bill is paid. As important as meeting current obligations is ensuring that the institution will be viable over the long run (Pocock 1984b).

This requirement complicates in at least two respects the board's role of budget approval. First, viewing resource management as an aspect of the board's role as preserver of the trust implies that resources will be applied to support institutional goals and purposes (Fisher 1969; Nelson 1980; Zwingle 1980a); therefore, responsible trustees will know the institution's goals and see that budget decisions support those goals, both in the short and the long run. In some instances, doing so might require the board to allow the institution to incur short-term debt to ready itself to meet long-term goals (Nason 1982). It certainly requires that the board establish the policies that will govern decisions about individual expenditures (Fisher 1969) and that it monitor expenditures regularly to ensure that the institution's goals are being supported (Pocock 1984b).

Second, the board has an obligation to consider more than just money as it makes budget decisions. In addition to funds, resources also take the form of land, facilities and equipment, support staff, and faculty, not all of which are readily exchangeable for funds (Nelson 1982). Hence, for example, decisions about personnel and academic programs, once made, carry continuing budgetary obligations that cannot readily be altered or abandoned. If, at the extreme, trustees are concerned only with balancing this year's budget while academic programs are added and faculty tenured thoughtlessly, future financial crisis may well ensue (Taylor 1984a).

The board's role as preserver of both current and future institutional vitality requires that trustees receive adequate information from administrators on which to base decisions about resources. "Adequacy" implies that information will be appropriate in depth and format to the needs of policy makers rather than administrators, that the assumptions underlying proposed decisions will be specified, that the reliability of the assumptions will be open to discussion and debate, and that information comparing the institution's financial situation to peers and to its own performance over time will be provided (Corson 1980; Nelson 1982; Taylor 1984a).

Trustees, presumably because many come from business backgrounds, are commonly thought to be well qualified to make financial judgments (Dorsey 1980; Radock and Jacobson 1980). Many trustees, however, particularly nonbusiness and newer board members, are overly deferential to those trustees seen as financial experts (Nason 1982; Pocock 1984b). And to the degree that administrators control the decisions about programs, facilities, and people that by extension determine where funds will be expended, administrators are frequently seen as equally or more powerful than boards in the financial sphere.

Develop and Preserve Physical Facilities
The board's responsibility for ensuring adequate physical facilities has historically been as well established as its roles in fund raising and budget approval. Founders and trustees of early colleges often secured land and buildings well before establishing programs or hiring a president (Rudolph 1962). Even now, trustees are often believed to be more comfortable with such worldly matters as land and buildings than with programs and faculty. Moreover, the board's responsibility for maintaining the trust is perhaps most visible in the institution's physical plant (Nason 1982).

Recently, the board's responsibility for preserving the physical plant has received new emphasis. The rapid expansion of institutions during the 1950s and 1960s saw buildings constructed rapidly and cheaply, and many of those structures are now deteriorating, more or less simultaneously. That it is occurring at a time of financial stringency for most institutions exacerbates the problem (Kaiser 1983, 1984).

To fulfill their role in developing and preserving facilities, trustees are advised to ensure that the institution adopt a master plan for campus facilities, specifying future needs for construction, demolition, and maintenance. Moreover, the board should determine appropriate levels of debt for the plant and establish conditions governing the acceptance of gifts of land or buildings and of grants to construct facilities. Such gifts or grants carry continuing financial obligations that the institution may not be able to afford (Nelson 1980). Finally, trustees are reminded that facilities exist to support programs and that facility-related decisions must be consonant with academic goals (Kaiser 1983; Nelson 1980).

Oversee Academic Affairs

The board's concern for academic affairs is considered to encompass four areas of responsibility: setting personnel policies and procedures for faculty, establishing academic programs, ensuring that budget decisions support academic priorities, and evaluating the institution's academic activities (Chait and associates 1984).

Such straightforward lists of responsibilities notwithstanding, much of what has been written about the board's role in academic affairs stresses the contradiction inherent in the role.

On the one hand, it is generally contended that trustees bear the ultimate and full responsibility for the performance of their institution. Simultaneously, faculties and administrators usually contend that trustees are not competent to make decisions as to admissions, faculty hiring and promotion, and what programs and courses should be offered. They should, in short, keep their fingers out of academic affairs (Corson 1973a, p. 6; see also Ruml and Morrison 1959).

Despite possible controversy, however, trustees are frequently advised that they have no choice but to become involved in academic matters. Budget decisions are seen as so intimately tied to academic policy that trustees cannot be involved in one without also tending to the other (Nelson 1979). As academic programs are the heart of the institution—and trustees are responsible for ensuring the institution's integrity—their responsibility for academic affairs is inescapable (Nason 1982). As a practical matter, trustees cannot be expected to support and promote decisions they have had no part in making (Dorsey 1980). And, finally, faculty are sometimes seen as little more competent than trustees to make broad educational policy. Faculty specialization and departmental initiative have promoted fractionated curricula, self-serving faculty personnel policies, and insufficient concern for the "whole" student (Corson 1975; Ruml and Morrison 1959).

Trustees are counseled to avoid routinely substituting their judgment for that of campus academic experts and are advised instead to oversee academic affairs largely by asking questions of faculty and administrators, evaluating the answers they receive, and then asking more questions if necessary (Association of American Colleges 1985; Chait and Taylor 1983; Corson 1980; Meyerson 1980). Such an approach is seen as consistent

with the constraints of the academic culture, which is characterized by diffuse power and expectations by faculty of considerable professional autonomy. In fact, it is argued with respect to
academic decision making that "the bedrock values of most
campus communities virtually demand that trustees participate
but not dictate" (Chait 1984, p. 9).

Trustees' responsible participation in academic affairs depends on familiarity with the institution, its programs, and its
distinctive values (Wood 1984b). Such familiarity is encouraged by formal and informal contacts between trustees and faculty, including faculty presentations to the board, faculty-
trustee dinners, joint meetings of parallel trustee and faculty academic affairs committees, ad hoc faculty-trustee committees to
study particular academic questions, and faculty membership on
board academic affairs committees (Chait and Taylor 1983;
Wood 1984b).

Appoint, Support, and Evaluate the President
Appointing the president is often described as the board's most
important responsibility (Bean 1975; Fisher 1969; Mortimer and
McConnell 1978; Nason 1982). A variation on this theme suggests that this responsibility is more accurately viewed as the
obligation to provide an effective *presidency*, that is, an office
that is attractive to highly qualified individuals and structured
to allow skillful leadership of the institution (Commission on
Strengthening 1984). In either case, the president is seen as the
key to the board's responsible performance, because it is the
president to whom the board delegates much of its authority
and to whom the board usually looks for guidance (Nason
1982).

Given the centrality and the significance of the president's
role, trustees are frequently advised to pay greater heed to the
process of selecting a president. In general, proposed improvements relate to defining explicitly what the institution requires
in a new president and being realistic in evaluating the abilities
of presidential candidates. Problems will arise later, it is argued, if the president is ill suited to the institution's needs or if
the board expects superhuman performance of the president
(American Council on Education/Association of Governing
Boards 1986; Munitz 1980).

The interdependence of boards and presidents frequently
leads to a description of the relationship as a partnership (Munitz 1980; Pray 1974). Boards are advised to appoint active pres-

idents and to give them the staff, authority, and support they need to be effective leaders (Carnegie Commission 1973a). The president is told that his or her leadership is strengthened by consultation with a board from which support and approval can be drawn (Corson 1980). Yet, as will be discussed later, the expectation of partnership is paradoxical; the board is expected both to support and to evaluate the president, roles that may conflict when the board and the president disagree over presidential performance (Wood 1985). And, at the same time, board members who rely on the president for their information and education are simultaneously expected to judge their teacher (Munitz 1980).

The potentially conflicting roles of supporter and evaluator tend to narrow the range of goals and devices for assessment boards are encouraged to adopt. First, the value of formal presidential evaluation is questioned. Such assessments, which are undertaken at regular intervals and which become public events as evidence is collected of presidential performance, are criticized for undermining presidential authority and prestige and for encouraging the president to do what is popular rather than what is right (Nason 1984).

A second apparent result of the paradox between support and evaluation is the suggestion that the purpose of the evaluation should be to improve rather than to penalize performance and that boards should evaluate presidents according to the achievement of the presidents' own goals (Munitz 1980; Nason 1984). Indeed, the president rather than the board should perhaps initiate the evaluation (Munitz 1980).

Finally, it is argued, presidential evaluations should be—and often are—expanded to encompass the board's performance. This step is a logical extension of the board-president partnership model, which presupposes that the two partners are interdependent (Munitz 1980; Nason 1984).

Arbitrate Internal Disputes
Short of intervention by courts or legislature, the board is the institution's final authority, and so it is charged with acting as a ''court of appeal'' when disputes arise (Nason 1982, p. 42). This role, always implicitly a trustee's responsibility, became more widely exercised during the turmoil of the 1960s and 1970s, when disagreements among campus constituencies erupted loudly and often (Perkins 1973).

Boards should ensure that codes and regulations governing

treatment and behavior of individuals are adopted, publicized, and followed and that appeals to the board are heard only after they have been pursued through established channels (Fisher 1969; Nason 1982).

Establish Goals and Evaluate Progress
If trustees are ultimately responsible for the viability and success of their institutions, success cannot be gauged except by reference to the achievement of goals. Hence, boards are responsible for participating in or at least being informed about institutional planning and evaluation (Bean 1975; Corson 1975; Dorsey 1980; Nason 1982; Pray 1974; Whitchead 1985).

It is sometimes argued that trustees are particularly suited to participate in planning because many are business people, and the business community in general is more comfortable with and sophisticated about planning than are most colleges and universities. Moreover, trustees with business backgrounds should be particularly familiar with issues of finances and facilities pertinent to planning (Bean 1975; Dorsey 1980). And trustees bring a detachment and a comprehensive sense of the institution to the planning process that other participants may lack (Nason 1982).

In contrast, other factors limit the potential of the trustee's role in planning. Trustees have too little time to be thoroughly involved, and they lack the academic expertise required to plan effectively. Hence, planning is properly left to administrators, and the board's responsibility is largely one of insisting that planning be done and done well (Dorsey 1980; Martin 1974; Zwingle 1980a).

A corollary to the board's responsibility for planning is its obligation to evaluate the institution's progress toward achieving its goals. Not only is it necessary to the institution's success, but it is also viewed as a means of preventing interference from outside groups' (courts, law makers, funding sources, and so on) needing assurance that the institution is well run (Bailey 1982; Ingram 1980b). As in planning, the board's detachment is seen as an advantage in evaluation (Corson 1975; Zwingle 1985), but trustees' lack of time and academic expertise suggests that the board's role should be to ensure that evaluation takes place rather than to serve as the evaluator (Chait and Taylor 1983; Meyerson 1980).

A special case in the discussion of evaluation is the board's role in institutional and specialized accreditation. Trustees have traditionally remained distant from the accreditation process (Ingram 1980b), but they are increasingly being advised to become informed about the purpose, process, and results of accreditation as one means of fulfilling their responsibility to evaluate (Association of Governing Boards Subcommittee 1982).

Act as Bridge and Buffer

It is sometimes argued that the board's central function is to link the institution with its environment, simultaneously representing the interests of society to the institution and vice versa (Aldrich 1979; Pfeffer and Salancik 1978). In addition to this function as a bridge, an expectation exists that trustees will buffer the institution from intrusion by the society (Nason 1982). If one assumes that the interests of society and the institution sometimes diverge, these roles may conflict, a situation that has created "a basic ambivalence in the role of the trustee that has not been resolved to this day" (Schenkel 1971, p. 9).

The trustee's role as a bridge from the institution to society is usually described as a public relations or government relations function. To perform this role, the trustee must understand the educational process and the institution's policies and be skillful in communicating with institutional constituencies, governmental agencies, and the general public (Cheit 1971; Fisher 1969; Ingram 1980b; Newman 1973; Ruml and Morrison 1959). This responsibility is viewed mainly as an ethical one, arising from the acceptance of a public trust, but it is also suggested that the failure to perform this aspect of the role as bridge will result in the loss of authority by the institution to governmental bodies and other external agencies (Corson 1975).

The board's function as buffer requires it to resist inappropriate intrusion by outside agencies into the internal affairs of the institution (Carnegie Commission 1973a). The role is a particularly nettlesome one for public institutions whose boards are often subject to direct pressure from governmental bodies and whose members may even view themselves as responsible more for transmitting than resisting intrusion (Pray 1975). For this reason, trustees from both the independent and the public sectors are encouraged to broaden their view of what constitutes accountability to the public interest, essentially raising it from the level of responding to immediate pressures to the higher plane of serving overarching societal goals (Mortimer and McConnell 1978; Newman 1973).

In fact, it is possible "that transmitting and resisting are not alternative strategies, but that [trustees], in yielding to some community pressures, might put themselves and the university in a better position to resist other, greater pressures" (Epstein 1974, p. 94).

Stimulate Change

Colleges and universities are essentially conservative institutions whose faculties resist change (Carnegie Commission 1973a; Ruml and Morrison 1959). While the appropriateness of the board's assuming the role of agent for change is controversial (Zwingle 1985), the board may be the only group sufficiently disinterested and yet informed to stimulate change (Carnegie Commission 1973a).

The appropriate role for the board may be that of prodder of administrators. The president of one university was reportedly galvanized into assuming the role of agent for change when a trustee asked him two questions: "What vision did he have for [the institution] ten years hence? And how did he plan to achieve that vision?" (Keller 1983, p. 95).

Act Responsibly

Trustees who act responsibly are well informed and comport themselves appropriately. Being informed "is a condition of the proper exercise of the [trustee's] other responsibilities," as, lacking information about their role and institution, trustees cannot hope to perform effectively (Nason 1982, p. 43).

Trustees are encouraged to seek information from any source (Gould 1973), to maintain between meetings an interest in the institution and in higher education (Zwingle 1985), and to bring a sense of curiosity to their work on the board (Corson 1980). In fact, the quest for information might require the board to have a staff of its own (Greenleaf 1974).

Board members who comport themselves appropriately adhere both in substance and in style to certain behavioral norms. In substance, the trustee is expected to act only as a member of the corporation, the trustee body as a whole, suggesting that the individual board member has no inherent authority to speak for the institution (Zwingle and Mayville 1974). It also reminds trustees of their obligation to act as a corporate body in the legal sense, placing the good of the institution before their personal interests (Lascell and Hallenbeck 1980). Among other responsibilities, trustees should avoid providing professional services to their institutions, a practice that could constitute a conflict of interest (Zwingle 1985). More fundamentally, it implies that trustees must attend meetings and participate knowledgeably in decision making (O'Connell 1985).

With respect to style, trustees are advised to conduct themselves with dignity and to show respect for those with differing opinions (Pray 1974). Once the board reaches a decision, that decision should have the support of the full board (Cheit 1971; Wessell 1974). Finally, trustees should remember that "influence decides more things than power" and that the board should avoid the blatant imposition of formal authority (Cheit 1971).

In sum, board members are advised that the obligation to act responsibly is not only an ethical necessity but also is the key to stemming the erosion of their authority and the loss of institutional autonomy to outside forces (Zwingle and Mayville 1974).

Considerable evidence suggests that boards do not always perform the roles they are advised to assume. A variety of factors, internal and external to the institution, appear to influence the nature of trustees' actual authority and the means by which it is exercised.

This chapter first examines a board's activity in policy making and administration and then explores three general propositions that may explain the roles boards actually undertake: (1) that trustees' ability to govern their institutions as they are advised to do is constrained by forces beyond their control; (2) that trustees choose not to exercise the authority attributed to them; and (3) that under certain conditions boards will assume responsibilities previously neglected.

Considerable evidence suggests that boards do not always perform the roles they are advised to assume.

Policy Making and Administration

As suggested earlier, trustees are usually advised that with few exceptions they should carry out their responsibilities by making policies and expecting administrators to execute them. A policy is "a general rule . . . or a statement of intent . . ., which provides guidance to administrators in reaching decisions with respect to . . . matters entrusted to their care" (Nelson 1985, p. 2). This division of responsibility arises from the board's legal obligation to manage the institution, even as its status as a nonresident, unpaid, lay body prevents it from providing day-to-day management (Kramer 1981; Wood 1984a).

Both in theory and in practice the policy/administration dichotomy is anything but clear. First, policy is a multilevel construct in which higher levels of policy govern the adoption of lower-level policies. One model defines three levels: *governing,* which are general policies set by boards relating to mission, educational program, and operations; *executive,* which are set by the president and other senior administrators to manage the institution's resources and operations consistent with governing policy; and *operating,* which are set by deans and directors in pursuit of executive policies (Bogue and Riggs 1974). "Administration" in this case may be conceived as a form of policy making (Paltridge, Hurst, and Morgan 1973).

A second model identifies six descending levels of policy, including *major* policies, which concern broad issues of mission and purpose; *secondary* policies, which relate to narrower but still crucial and uncommon matters, such as adding a new academic department; *functional* policies, which govern the regular operations of an institution and include, for example, the adoption of an annual operating budget; *minor* policies, which include "essentially procedural matters [that] are elevated in importance" because they are controversial or arise infrequently; *procedures and standard operating plans*, which direct the daily activities of various offices and departments; and *rules*, which include very specific regulations governing campus parking and the like (Wood 1985, p. 129).

In both models, policy levels are mutually influencing. The influence of higher on lower levels of policy is illustrated in the decisions of the Harvard Corporation (its governing board) in the 1940s to make Harvard a "national" college and by the New York City Board of Higher Education in the 1970s to establish an open admissions policy for the City University of New York. Both decisions produced "radical" changes in curriculum and academic climate, which in turn were governed by myriad lower-level policy decisions (Martin 1974, pp. 5–6).

These examples are consistent with the general wisdom suggesting that, as protectors of institutions' long-term welfare, boards should operate at the higher levels of policy making where overriding concerns are addressed. For example, decisions about institutional mission and the adoption of the annual budget are consistently judged to be board business (Commission on Strengthening 1984; Lewis 1980; Nelson 1985). And even in areas like academic affairs, where faculty claim special expertise, trustees are advised that they remain obligated to promulgate high-level, overriding policies (Chait and associates 1984).

Higher-level policy is often governed by previously made lower-level decisions, however, whether by necessity or chance or in an attempt to control the eventual outcome of the board's deliberations. For example, the appointment of faculty members with particular skills, the development of individual courses, the decision to spend even modest amounts of money on one initiative rather than another, and myriad other operational decisions may constrain the board's subsequent policy decisions. In other words, a "great mass of policy is formed by operational imperatives and filters to the top, where the board is more or less forced to accept it" (Pray 1975, p. 21).

The relative knowledge and experience of administrators and trustees appear to be factors here. "The staff has to educate the board constantly and persistently, and it certainly does choose the elements of education [that] lead toward the conclusion of which the staff approves. In other words, we tell them how to

vote and we call that process 'the board sets . . . policy' "
(Auerbach 1961, p. 68; see also Middleton 1983; Price 1963).
Stated somewhat less dogmatically, "Many of the initiatives
for which trustees take credit appear to have existed in embry-
onic form within the administration or to have had such wide
currency that trustees and senior staff may have picked up an
idea almost simultaneously" (Wood 1985, p. 142).

A board's operating style also appears to influence its involvement in policy making (Wood 1985, pp. 94–115). A *ratifying* board tends to accept administrative judgments
unquestioningly and so would be expected to act as the prover-
bial rubber stamp in the policy-making process. This board is
one that believes its main responsibility is to hire a president
and then let him or her run the institution. A *corporate* board,
in contrast, involves itself in the sort of financial and managerial matters that are seen in business organizations but generally
expects the president to assume complete administrative authority for the institution. And trustees on a *participatory* board frequently involve themselves directly in the administration of the
institution, usually out of a sense of personal ownership and responsibility for its affairs. Not surprisingly, most members of
participatory boards in independent institutions are alumni.

> *The way presidents handle the policy structure with their
> boards seems less a function of certainty about what a policy
> issue really is than a defensive tactic for dealing with the
> board's operating style. . . . A president with a participa-
> tory board will find that if the board is to remain satisfied, it
> must become involved in issues [that] a corporate board
> might consider administrative* (Wood 1985, p. 134).

Perhaps it is for this reason that many boards appear to be
more deeply involved in making specific managerial decisions
than in making or approving policies (Corson 1980; Lee and
Bowen 1971; Odendahl and Boris 1983).

At least two studies suggest that trustees wish to share authority for institutional policy making with administrators and
faculty members. In the first, fewer than two-thirds of some
275 trustees of public and independent colleges and universities
reported that their boards would assume final authority for
changing the institution's mission or for evaluating the president's performance. Fewer than one-half of the respondents indicated that their boards would decide matters concerning the

establishment of faculty tenure, promotion, compensation, or retirement policies, or the establishment or discontinuation of academic programs. In each case, respondents reported relying significantly on administrators to take action on these and other matters typically considered board responsibilities (Taylor 1984b, pp. 38–42). A second study demonstrated trustees' clear preference for sharing major authority with administrators and sometimes faculty members for establishing faculty personnel policies, tuition levels, and degree programs (Rauh 1969, pp. 38–39).

Depending on the nature of the shared authority, this position is not necessarily a violation of what is considered good board practice. Although boards are advised to rely on the professional expertise of faculty and administrators, they may be said to be shirking their responsibility for participating knowledgeably in all major institutional decisions to the extent that they serve merely to provide legal sanction for administrative and faculty initiatives.

With respect to the matter of the board's involvement in managerial detail, a survey of 400 business executives serving on nonprofit boards is instructive. Board members' most common roles were fund raising, establishing operating procedures, enlisting support from others, budgeting and fiscal control, and providing a different point of view to the organization. Note that neither "supervising management" nor "formulating broad policy" is included in this list. When respondents were asked what they would like to do on their boards, they most frequently listed "deciding on operating procedures and public relations strategies" and "carrying out assignments given to them by administrators" (Middleton 1983, pp. 10–11).

Many nonprofit organizations have fewer and less sophisticated staff to rely on than most college and university boards have, and so perhaps these findings are to be expected. But a study of 20 boards of four-year public colleges and universities reached somewhat similar conclusions. This research (Paltridge, Hurst, and Morgan 1973) classified board decisions by three levels: I—*legislative*, II—*managerial*, and III—*working*. Legislative decisions deal with ethical principles, general rules, and long-range issues; managerial decisions concern organizational control, direction of subordinates, and interpretation of legislative policy; and working decisions relate to the implementation of specific rules and procedures. The study found that of nearly 4,000 individual board decisions, approximately 42 percent were classified as level III and 38 percent level II. In contrast, less than 8 percent of the decisions were classified as level I, at which boards are in theory expected to operate (p. 38). This pattern remained fairly consistent across the four types of boards studied (comprehensive state, multicampus, single institution with subsidiary branch campuses, and single campus), despite variations in their authority to make level I decisions (pp. 56–62).

This finding is particularly disturbing to observers of multicampus boards who note that trustees often engage in detailed decision making as if they were governing one campus rather than several. And they usually do so without the benefit of intimate knowledge of the affected campus. This practice undermines one of the primary justifications for multicampus boards: that they can concern themselves with universitywide policy and leave managerial details to the campuses (Lee and Bowen 1971).

Involvement of this sort in low-level policy making and execution may be seen with particular frequency among trustees whose knowledge of such matters as real estate, financial investments, or law rivals or exceeds that of an institution's administration (Nelson 1985). Trustees who are reluctant to become involved in broad, long-term issues but who do not want to be labeled "rubber stamps" can thus assume the role of "expert consultant." By providing what amounts to professional advice, trustees feel they are contributing needed expertise to the institution and are able to see concrete results from their work (Wood 1985, p. 145).

Particularly among independent colleges and universities, individuals who provide professional services to institutions are quite frequently members of the board. For example, 26 percent of these boards include the institution's designated legal counsel, 17 percent the president of the bank where the institution does all or most of its business, and 10 percent the institution's primary financial advisor (Taylor 1987). These statistics, because they include only those services officially rendered, doubtless understate the full extent of consultative services provided.

The consulting role is problematic for two reasons. First, it "often leaves unrealized the strategic and developmental perspectives a governing board is uniquely able to foster" (Wood 1985, p. 145). Second, it may violate the trustee's obligation to avoid potential conflicts of interest.

Constraints on Trustees' Ability to Govern
The nature of colleges and universities as organizations
Perhaps the most fundamental factors affecting trustees' ability to govern concern the nature of colleges and universities as organizations and the limitations these organizational features pose for the exercise of formal authority.

Colleges and universities are variously described as *bureaucratic, collegial*, or *political* organizations (Baldridge, Curtis, and Riley 1978). The bureaucratic model presupposes an organization structured to achieve specific goals with maximum efficiency. To that end, the organization is conceived as a hierarchy with clear lines of authority, an emphasis on competence as the criterion for appointment and promotion of officials, and reliance on formal channels of communication and on formal policies and regulations to guide organizational processes.

While this model has features that explain certain structural aspects of college and university governance (Stroup 1966), it falls far short of describing the actual decision processes observed in most institutions. It fails, for example, to account for the use of power and informal authority through threats, expertise, and appeals to emotion, and, while it describes the implementation of policies, it is inadequate to account for the process of policy formulation (Baldridge, Curtis, and Riley 1978).

The collegial model of the college or university rests on a view of the institution as a community in which policy making and management are undertaken with the full participation and consent of the community—particularly the faculty. Much of the justification for the model derives from the observation that professionals within a bureaucracy—college and university faculty members, for example—tend "to develop a different sort of structure from that characteristic of the administrative hierarchy [of a bureaucracy]. Instead . . . there tends to be what is roughly, in formal status, a company of equals" (Parsons 1947, p. 60).

A serious limitation of the literature describing the collegial model is its failure to distinguish between the descriptive and normative views of the approach. *Is* the university a collegium or *ought* it to be one? In fact, much collegial decision making occurs on many campuses, but other decisions are highly contested and "the consensus [that results] actually represents the prevalence of one group over another" (Baldridge, Curtis, and Riley 1978, p. 34).

Much of the literature on trusteeship supports the collegial view to the extent of suggesting that boards should defer to the judgment of faculty, particularly in academic matters. Effective and enthusiastic teaching is seen as inseparable from academic freedom and related issues of control over faculty hiring, development of curriculum, and selection of teaching methods (Mortimer and McConnell 1978; Ruml and Morrison 1959). The authoritarianism that may suit a business is incompatible with the diffusion of authority necessary to enable faculty to perform the institution's central academic functions (Besse 1973; Corson 1973b). In summary, trustees are told, the campus is not a democracy but neither is the professional task of the faculty compatible with strictly hierarchical methods of governance (Carnegie Commission 1973a).

The political model of higher education governance assumes that the institution may be conceived as a political system in which various individuals and groups compete for the right to make policy decisions. Thus, the board is seen as one of several constituents rather than the apex of an institutional hierarchy or the facilitator of consensus.

Several assumptions about the organization underlie the model (Baldridge, Curtis, and Riley 1978, pp. 35–36). First, inactivity prevails because most constituents (including trustees) are uninterested in most of the decisions being made at any given time. Administrators, in particular, become by default the primary decision makers.

Second, because of this low level of interest in many decisions, participation in the decision-making process is fluid; the right to make a decision usually adheres to those who persist.

Third, the institution is fragmented into interest groups. The aims of faculty, trustees, administrators, and other internal and external constituents are likely to differ because their goals for the institution are usually vaguely articulated and often at odds.

Fourth, because goals differ, conflict is normal and in fact can lead to healthy change within the organization. Trustees are often uncomfortable with this reality, though they are cautioned to anticipate and even welcome conflict. The institution is described as "a battleground of ideas" where a "clear responsibility for trustees is to make sure there *are* differences, competent disagreements, fervid confrontations" (Martin 1974, pp. 2–3; see also Meyerson 1980; Wood 1984a).

Fifth, fragmentation of interest groups and resulting conflicts lead to the observation that formal authority is limited. The nearly absolute authority given to trustees in charters and organizational charts is curtailed as other interest groups bring pressures to bear. This case is particularly true in academic matters where faculty expertise frequently leads trustees to exercise virtually no authority over the institution's most fundamental functions (Besse 1973).

Finally, the model suggests, external interest groups are important. Government agencies, legislatures, courts, benefactors, prospective students, and others exert direct or indirect influence over the institution's policies and policy-making practices. Formal authority in the hands of trustees may be no match for external pressures, which can be particularly acute during periods of reduction and demographic decline (Carnegie Commission 1973a).

In sum, while many noncontroversial issues in colleges and universities may be decided collegially or through established bureaucratic procedures, the political model is perhaps most pertinent for describing decision making in an organization with vague and conflicting goals, a professoriate with considerable informal authority, and an environment positioned to make powerful claims on the institution. In other words, boards cannot govern alone because, despite the language of charters, they are not the sole repositories of authority in colleges and universities.

Decline of influence

We have seen that historically trustees' authority has declined as professional expertise of faculty and administrators has increased and become more important to institutional success. Trustees, it is argued,

> simply do not have the time, the experience, or the knowledge to govern much of the large and complex institution for which they are legally responsible. Nor is there any way, compatible with the traditional conception of trusteeship, for board members to acquire the time, experience, or knowledge (Epstein 1974, p. 90).

The paradox seems to be that the attributes that enable trustees to perform their functions as bridge and buffer and thus to legitimate the institution in the eyes of the public are the very qualities that prevent board members from exercising authority over the institution based on competence (Price 1963).

Administrators, particularly the president, often dominate board decision making by controlling the flow of information to trustees and by bringing only "safe" and minor issues to the board's attention (Kramer 1965, p. 111). And, because trustees report that the president is not only their chief but also their most trusted source of information (Taylor 1984b, pp. 28–32), it is unlikely that many trustees will demand that the board's role be broadened. Moreover, it is difficult to retrieve power once delegated because those to whom it has been given come to believe that the delegated authority is theirs by right (Corson 1973a).

Delegation of authority to presidents by boards of some multicampus systems appears particularly extensive. Constraints on time, complexity of the system, and geographic distance from individual campuses are among the explanations for the increased influence attributed to these presidents (Epstein 1974; Millett 1984; Munitz 1981).

Some observers point out that because the board retains the ability to dismiss the president, it continues to exert considerable influence, even when the president appears to dominate the board's activity (Zald 1969). Thus it seems that an implicit agreement may be struck between the board and the president: The board will delegate broad authority to the president, even at the risk of appearing to be a rubber stamp, but ultimately if displeased will remove the president (Munitz 1980; Trow 1984). It is argued, however, "the limitation is that [trustees] cannot use the power [to dismiss the president] very often without becoming ridiculous and reducing university administration to a shambles" (Epstein 1974, p. 93).

Delegation of authority to presidents by boards of some multicampus systems appears particularly extensive.

Changing institutional values

The 19th century college "was a unit . . . held together by a clearly perceived and accepted purpose, by a coherent curriculum, and by [cohesive] professional and social relationships" (Ruml and Morrison 1959, p. 48]. Several influences contributed to the breakdown of this unity: specialization of knowledge, the introduction of the elective system, changing motivation for attending college, institutions' growing size and complexity, the politicization of higher education, and shortages in resources, among others (Carnegie Commission 1973b; Corson 1973a; Nason 1982; Ruml and Morrison 1959).

These influences, which continue to affect American colleges and universities, also constrain trustees' ability to govern.

Trustees are left unsure of their role. Are they to be statesmen, exercising independent judgments, or representatives, reflecting the views of constituents? (Jones 1985). Statesmanship requires general consensus about the institution's purposes and a willingness by members of the public and the academic community to accept trustees' authority—conditions notably lacking in most institutions (Corson 1973a; Epstein 1974; Nason 1982; Newman 1973).

Alternatively, if trustees decide to represent constituents, they undermine the most fundamental conception of their roles as stewards of a larger public trust. Moreover, they ultimately risk the demise of trusteeship itself because the "logical terminus [of the politicization of institutions] is the elimination of intermediary authorities" (Jones 1985, p. 15).

External influences

As the political model suggests, the ability of a board of trustees to govern is constrained by a variety of factors external to the institution. As higher education has assumed greater importance to American society, external control, particularly of public institutions, has increased to the point that institutional independence and privilege have declined dramatically (Carnegie Commission 1973b; Corson 1970). And even independent institutions, to the degree that they are affected by external regulations, economic and demographic trends, and changing public attitudes, cannot entirely chart their destinies (Baldridge, Curtis, and Riley 1978; Mortimer and McConnell 1978).

Public control. Governmental authorities are "everywhere enmeshed" in the governance of public campuses (Lee and Bowen 1971, p. 117). This involvement "has become, over the long term, both less and more intrusive—less in the old-fashioned political sense . . . more in the sense of bureaucratic surveillance and controls" (Commission on Strengthening 1984, p. 81). Moreover, 60 percent of public campuses and 67 percent of public college students are part of multicampus institutions (Association of Governing Boards 1986, p. 19). Such institutions, as we shall see, present special challenges to traditional systems of governance.

Governments' interest in higher education stems from several sources. Institutions are seen as crucial to economic development (Education Commission of the States 1986; Millett 1984; Newman 1986), while at the same time states are concerned about declining enrollments, program quality and coordination, financing and student aid, and relations between the public and independent sectors (Kauffman 1980; Millett 1984).

States have developed a wide range of structures and practices intended to ensure that their interests in higher education are represented and protected. A state may have a separate governing board for each public institution, a governing board for a system of senior institutions and a system of two-year colleges, a statewide governing board for all public institutions, or some combination (Millett 1984, p. 239). In addition, a state may have a coordinating agency with specific authority over the governing boards of public and/or independent institutions (Berdahl 1971).

By 1972, "47 states had established either consolidated governing boards responsible for all senior institutions (and in some cases, community and junior colleges also) or coordinating boards responsible for statewide planning and coordination of two or more governing boards" (Education Commission of the States 1986, p. 1). The ensuing years have seen a continuation of this pattern as well as a "major increase" in the involvement of legislative staffs and executive branch agencies in higher education (p. 1).

State governing boards at their best are seen as a means of ensuring that institutions serve multiple goals efficiently and that diversity among campuses is fostered (Lavine 1980; Lee and Bowen 1971). In addition, such boards are seen as preferable to the more extensive direct control by state governments that would likely result without the board as a buffer (Lee and Bowen 1975; Newman 1986).

These strengths are not endemic to the multicampus board structure, however. The effectiveness of such boards depends more on the prestige and skill of individual board members, their ability to function as a unit, and the reputation of their staffs among institutional and governmental officials (Education Commission of the States 1986). Moreover, the ability of these boards to focus on broad policy rather than on administrative detail is seen as a key to effectiveness (Newman 1986).

Statewide and other multicampus governing boards do not want for detractors. State officials criticize them for being overly identified with institutional rather than with state interests (Millett 1984), but too often this identification translates into the same preoccupation with detailed decision making that permeates boards of single-campus institutions (Commission on

Strengthening 1984; Lee and Bowen 1971; Paltridge, Hurst, and Morgan 1973).

In other instances, far from failing to represent state interests, critics charge that multicampus state boards actually transmit political pressure, particularly where government officials serve ex officio on governing boards (McConnell 1971). Moreover, a multicampus structure may be more efficiently dominated by government officials who must deal with just one board rather than several (Lee and Bowen 1971).

In states where public universities have been established by constitution, such institutions are theoretically more insulated from political pressure than universities established by law and vulnerable to legislative action (Cheit 1971). In fact, particularly because it depends on the legislature for funds, the board of a constitutional university may not be able to fend off threats to its autonomy (Mortimer and McConnell 1978; Newman 1986).

Rather than protecting diversity, state and other multicampus boards are often seen as exerting a leveling influence by promulgating rigid rules and procedures that reduce institutional autonomy and diversity (Carnegie Foundation 1976; Kauffman 1980).

Finally, that the rise of multicampus boards has meant the decline of individual campus boards is troubling to some. An institution lacking its own board is denied the benefits of a lay group knowledgeable about and committed only to it (Kauffman 1980; Millett 1984; Sweet 1980).

Open meeting laws. Eighty-eight percent of public boards of trustees and 62 percent of their standing committees are required by law to meet in public (Taylor 1987). Some believe this practice demystifies the board's role, gives interested parties a chance to be heard, and prevents casual and misguided decision making (Cleveland 1985; Ingram 1980b; Rauh 1973). Critics charge, however, that candor is sacrificed in open meetings, that discussion is oversimplified to avoid misunderstanding, and that the most important issues may not be discussed at all. In fact, many significant decisions are made by the president or others in the institution because the board is too constrained to discuss them fully (Cleveland 1985).

Finally, laws requiring public meetings are thought to damage presidential search and evaluation processes by discouraging strong candidates from being considered, by impeding candor in search and evaluation, and by opening the processes to political manipulation (Cleveland 1985; Commission on Strengthening 1984).

Environmental dependence. The influence of trustees as individuals or as a corporate body may be conceived as a function of their ability to "cope with critical organizational uncertainties" (Pfeffer and Salancik 1978, p. 167). If board members provide crucial resources or are linked to important external groups that provide funding or legitimation, they are likely to be more influential within the institution (Zald 1969). To the degree that funding comes from public sources, whether to public or independent institutions, the board's authority over significant issues such as mission and budget is likely to be sacrificed to external agencies (Baldridge, Curtis, and Riley 1978; Carnegie Foundation 1982).

One study of nonprofit social service organizations in four countries found that in situations where the government had provided substantial funding to the organizations, trustees' influence declined accordingly. Where trustees were seen as crucial in obtaining funds, however, board members retained considerable power (Kramer 1981).

Nearly 20 years ago, a major study concluded that the great majority of trustees contributed less than $2,000 per year to their institutions, whether public or independent (Rauh 1969, p. 178). A more recent survey (Taylor 1987) concluded that trustees' giving has increased substantially, particularly in independent institutions, but arguably still not enough to rank the board a primary source of institutional funds. Nor, as a study of small, independent, liberal arts colleges indicated, do trustees report being deeply involved in raising large gifts from others. Trustees in this instance expect the president to serve as the primary fund raiser (Wood 1985, p. 79). Trustees may be more influential than they believe, however, making the occasional, "presumably effortless, telephone call to provide the president with entrée" that he or she might not otherwise obtain (p. 142).

The board's authority is constrained in complex, high-quality, relatively wealthy institutions because trustees exert less influence over such critical resources as research dollars, the pool of student applicants, and the legitimation of the institution by significant outsiders (Baldridge, Curtis, and Riley 1978; Zald 1969).

Public boards, for example, particularly those of two-year and comprehensive four-year institutions, are far less likely than independent boards to delegate detailed authority for decision making to administrators (Hartnett 1969; Taylor 1984b). These boards are politically appointed or popularly elected and therefore an important source of legitimation and public support for their institutions. This situation is particularly apparent when these institutions lack sufficient prestige to attract countervailing legitimation from alternative sources. The ability of these boards to engage in detailed decision making is enhanced by their tendencies to meet three times more frequently than independent boards and to reside nearer their institutions (Rauh 1969; Taylor 1987).

Declining to Govern

It appears that some boards are not only constrained by others in their efforts to govern but that they also seek to limit their own involvement in important institutional affairs. First, few board members spend much time on their trusteeships; a sample of over 5,000 trustees reported giving an average of just 63 hours per year to various trustee-related activities, including attending meetings. Not surprisingly, public trustees, who attend more meetings and are more involved in detailed decision making, spend more time on trusteeship than independent trustees do (Hartnett 1969, p. 41; Taylor 1987).

A recent study of 10 independent liberal arts colleges indicated that trustees vary widely in the amount of time they spend on board duties, the most active giving an average of one and one-half days per month in addition to scheduled meetings and the least active doing nothing but attending meetings, if that (Wood 1985, p. 59).

Trustees may purposely give most attention to those institutional affairs with which they feel comfortable, usually finance and physical plant (Corson 1973a; Jencks and Riesman 1968). Together, these two areas accounted for 45 percent of the formal actions taken in 1972 by a sample of 14 public boards, though it is noteworthy that these boards also gave greater attention in that year than they had in 1964 to decisions affecting academic programs (Paltridge, Hurst, and Morgan 1973, p. 31). Nevertheless, the board's discomfort with academic affairs, combined with the inclination of many administrators and faculty members to protect professional hegemony over the educational program, suggest it is unlikely that many boards will insist on making educational decisions to the neglect of financial affairs and matters involving the physical plant (Corson 1980).

As we have seen, many board members are motivated, at least in part, by the prestige and visibility associated with their trusteeship (Auerbach 1961). This observation leads some to conclude that boards may decline to govern because "they would gain little from the eruption of conflict and controversy [that] then might become public and threaten their prestige" (Middleton 1983, p. 26). An aversion to conflict seems particularly evident among self-perpetuating boards with high-status members who "share the general upper-middle class allergy for 'trouble' of whatever sort" (Jencks and Riesman 1968, p. 16; see also Middleton 1983, p. 42).

Reclaiming the Authority to Govern

A board's authority is not necessarily constant over time. During periods of important organizational change or crisis, boards are likely to become more active (Hartnett 1970; Zald 1969). Financial, legal, and identity problems are now fairly common among institutions, leading to a pervasive sense that boards are beginning to reassert themselves (Baldridge, Curtis, and Riley 1978; Ingram 1980b; Kerr and Gade 1986).

A series of case studies of small, independent colleges that had encountered and recovered from severe financial crisis (Chaffee 1984) reveals a pattern among several of the institutions of the board's lethargy before the point at which the crisis could no longer be ignored, followed by the board's involvement, which helped save the institutions. Trustees of those colleges fired presidents, gave and raised funds, rallied community support, legitimated the institution to creditors, and on occasion stepped in to provide temporary day-to-day management. In most of these institutions, trustees had earlier been complacent and arguably had contributed to the crises they later acted to help solve. "All too frequently institutions are caught by surprise . . . in a crisis that only seems to be a sudden development" (Zwingle 1980a, p. 419).

Not all increased board activity is associated with recovery from financial crisis. As noted earlier, the board's support and influence have also been related to the achievement of significant gains in institutional quality among already stable institutions (Gilley, Fulmer, and Reithlingshoefer 1986).

The increased involvement of the governing board that results from financial stress seems to be more managerial than policy oriented, consistent with the observation that when organizations are in trouble, they centralize authority in an attempt to strengthen their response to external pressure. As they do so, however, boards may neglect major policy matters in the face of day-to-day administrative pressures. Over time, the board's role of leadership deteriorates and is difficult to reestablish (Cheit 1971).

In contrast, the behavior of the board associated with gains in quality among healthy institutions appears to be focused on policy, supportive of the president, and oriented toward legitimating the institution to the external environment (Gilley, Fulmer, and Reithlingshoefer 1986).

Summary
While boards are advised to develop or at least participate in developing most important institutional policies, evidence suggests that they are more likely to involve themselves in the operating details of colleges and universities.

Several explanations for this observation have been tendered. First, it is often difficult to distinguish policy making from administration and virtually impossible, given the range of policy matters to be decided, to assign all responsibility for making policy to trustees. The knowledge and experience of administrators, traditions of faculty authority over academic and allied matters, the board's operating style, and the realities of environmental dependence appear to influence the actual exercise of the board's authority. Moreover, trustees may in effect decline to govern by giving little time to their trusteeships and by dealing with less controversial matters to avoid conflict. In this case, trustees' activities often take the form of expert consultation on operational matters.

Increased activity of the board appears to be associated with recovery from institutional financial crisis as well as with the achievement of significant gains in quality in basically healthy colleges and universities. In the former case, the activity tends to be operational, while in the latter it is largely supportive of administrators and externally oriented.

BOARD STRUCTURE AND PROCESSES

In effect, colleges and universities are corporations established by charter, legislation, or constitution that vest governing boards with responsibility for carrying out the institution's purposes (Zwingle 1985, p. 7). The board's bylaws describe its responsibilities, structure, and processes (Ingram 1980a).

Board Structure

The board's formal structure consists of its officers and committees (Rauh 1973). Typically, a board's officers include a chair, who presides at meetings, and a vice chair, who serves in the absence of the chair.

The positions of secretary and treasurer of the board, once positions held by trustees, are now frequently occupied by full-time institutional staff. The secretary in this case is usually charged with providing staff assistance to the board and liaison with the office of the president. The treasurer is the chief financial officer of the institution. Along with the president, these board officers and administrators are referred to either as officers of the board or of the institution, leading in some cases to confusion over whether secretaries and treasurers are responsible to the board or to the president. Most observers claim that staff should not report directly to the board, because this practice tends to undercut the president's authority (Ingram 1980a; Rauh 1973).

The board chair

The chair's recommended job description usually includes the responsibilities to guide and protect the president and to lead and manage the board. With respect to the president, the chair is advised to be a supportive, available sounding board. The president should be able to turn to the chair concerning problems with working and living arrangements or intrusions on presidential prerogatives from trustees, institutional constituents, or outsiders (Pocock 1984a).

Open, frank, informal discussions over lunch, dinner, or the telephone, whether or not they involve matters of substance, are said to strengthen the tie between the chair and the president (Pocock 1984a; Whitehead 1985). In fact, a study of the relationship between chair and president concluded that the quality of personal interaction between the two was the single greatest determinant of the relationship's success (Cleary 1980).

The chair's responsibilities for board management and leadership include the responsibility to set a good example for other

A study of the relationship between chair and president concluded that the quality of personal interaction between the two was the single greatest determinant of the relationship's success.

trustees and the willingness to intercede and help solve disputes within the board. The chair should speak for the board with the knowledge of the president and should be willing on behalf of the board to accept public responsibility for controversial decisions apt to prove problematic for the president (Nason 1982; Pocock 1984a).

The chair is charged with ensuring that the board addresses the right issues in a timely manner with benefit of appropriate background information. To that end, the chair is advised to become knowledgeable about higher education, guided both by the president and by outside contacts and sources of information (Pocock 1984a), implying that the board and the institution are best served by a chair who is the president's partner but not his or her captive.

In actuality, the leadership roles chairs assume vary considerably, depending on the board's traditions, the attitudes of the president, and the inclinations of the chair. Some see themselves primarily as the president's supporter and advisor, some as mediators among board members and between the board and the president, some as educational leaders with personal visions for their institutions, and others as virtual copresidents, actively involved in the daily affairs of the institution (Rauh 1973; Wood 1985).

Common barriers to the exercise of leadership by chairs include the part-time nature of their commitment and the functional authority of the president, whom most trustees consider to be the board's primary leader (Pocock 1984a; Wood 1985). Asked in a study of boards' effectiveness to assess the influence of selected factors on boards' decision making, approximately twice as many trustees attributed "considerable influence" to the president's recommendations than ascribed similar influence to guidance by the chair. Moreover, such factors as guidance by committees and first-hand knowledge of the situation were more often seen as influential than leadership by the chair (Davis and Batchelor 1974, p. 23).

It has been suggested that the chair cannot be effective without professional training, a major commitment of time, and perhaps even a salary (Greenleaf 1974). This arrangement has been tried rarely and has usually worked poorly. The institution "ends up with two full-time administrators, and the division of labor between a Mr. Inside (president) and a Mr. Outside (chairman), plausible as it looks on paper and in theory, rarely works out well in practice" (Nason 1982, p. 85).

Nevertheless, chairs tend to devote more time to trusteeship than other board members do (Pocock 1984a). A few have offices on campus designated for their exclusive use—8 percent of chairs in the public sector and 3 percent in the independent sector—implying that they spend enough time on board business to warrant needing space (Taylor 1987).

The chair's broad theoretical role, combined with a willingness to spend time and a talent for directing, can lead to a variation on the "inner board" problem often associated with executive committees: The chair dominates and the rest of the board feels disenfranchised (O'Connell 1985; Rauh 1969). Long terms in office probably encourage the inclination of some chairs to dominate their boards, presidents, and institutions. "The special position of authority, the inside knowledge, the intimate relation with the president" can lead to a "slightly proprietary attitude" (Nason 1982, p. 84).

To prevent such problems, specific limitations on chairs' terms of office have been suggested, but such arbitrary rules can create difficulties as well as solve them. It takes time to build a relationship with the president and to become knowledgeable about the board's responsibilities and the intricacies of the institution. Moreover, few members of any board have the time, talent, and inclination to serve as chair. Why purposely turn out of office an effective chair and replace him or her with someone who may be less talented and more reluctant to serve? (Pocock 1984a).

In fact, relatively few boards—approximately one-fifth in both public and independent sectors—limit the number of years the chair may serve in that capacity. Where limits exist, they are higher in independent institutions than in the public sector (five versus three years). On average, incumbent chairs in independent institutions have served longer than their counterparts in the public sector (four versus three years), but neither has served very long (Taylor 1987). Thus, the trustee who has occupied the chair long enough to be considered a near-permanent resident seems, currently at least, to be a rarity.

Standing committees

Standing committees are part of the board's structure in 85 percent of public institutions and 98 percent of independent colleges and universities. Committees frequently include nontrustees as members, particularly faculty and students from the institution (Taylor 1987), which is considered an effective means of enhancing communication between the board and its constituents without the disadvantages attributed to faculty's and students' membership on the board (Ingram 1980a; Pray 1974).

Committees are said to perform one or any combination of the following functions:

1. To accomplish more business than the full board alone can
2. To educate trustees about specific institutional problems
3. To use the skills of individual trustees
4. To provide for greater contact between trustees and staff members
5. To take advantage of the proximity of local trustees in cases where most board members live far from campus
6. To screen matters for consideration by the full board (Rauh 1973, p. 234).

A study of trustees' and presidents' perceptions of the board's effectiveness concluded that, second only to recommendations of the president, trustees believe that strong guidance by committees is the most influential factor in the board's decision making (Davis and Batchelor 1974, p. 23). This finding suggests that trustees may do what they consider their most significant work in committee and by extension sheds further light on what board members define as useful activity.

As suggested earlier, "Trustees like to think of themselves as a panel of consultants with diverse fields of expertise. . . . Most often, the committee structure is the vehicle through which trustees channel their expertise" (Wood 1985, p. 69). Thus, the inclination of many boards to engage in detailed decision making rather than broad formulation of policy (Paltridge, Hurst, and Morgan 1973) profits from trustees' activities on committees.

A board's committee structure tends to resemble the institution's administrative organization. That is, some of the committees found most commonly include academic affairs, student affairs, fund raising, finance, and buildings and grounds (Taylor 1987). Committee agendas "tend to mirror the activities of the functional vice presidents" and usually include short-term issues and relatively minor policy matters, such as approvals by a finance committee of an increase in employees' health benefits and by an academic affairs committee of a list of recommendations for faculty members' sabbatical leaves (Wood 1985, p. 131). Not surprisingly, such functional committees depend to a great extent on the institution's staff for information and recommendations (Taylor 1984b; Wood 1985).

As a rule, trustees believe that some committees are more important than others. Finance, development, and investment are the committees with higher status, while assignments to committees on academic and student affairs, for example, are considered less desirable (Auerbach 1961; Wood 1985). The board's authority over financial matters has been less contested than that exercised over educational affairs, and trustees' professional backgrounds often make them more comfortable with and interested in worldly rather than academic questions (Corson 1980; Rauh 1973; Wood 1985).

The extent to which trustees and their committees feel comfortable in exercising authority over various aspects of institutional affairs is also evident in the composition of committees. Committees on academic and student affairs are far more likely to include faculty and student representatives than are committees on finance and investment (Taylor 1987), reflecting the general sentiment by trustees that constituents should have a say in matters that affect them and indicating that trustees feel less expert in nonfinancial matters (Corson 1980; Rauh 1969).

Committees' membership and leadership can encourage or discourage contributions by individual committee members. When the board's greatest expert on a given topic chairs a related committee or is too readily deferred to by other committee members, the expert trustee may intimidate or discourage broad participation (Chait and Taylor 1983; O'Connell 1985). Similarly, when committee chairs serve for long periods, they may exert so much influence that other trustees are disinclined to participate actively in a committee's affairs (Wood 1985).

As noted, committees are found more frequently in independent than in public institutions. This difference probably has less to do with institutional control per se than with the differences in size of boards and frequency of meetings associated with control. Public boards have an average of 11 members and meet nine times per year, while independent boards have 32 members and meet just four times annually (Taylor 1987). Therefore, public boards—particularly those of two-year colleges, which average nine members and meet monthly (Taylor 1987)—are more likely to function as committees of the whole (Ingram 1980a; Pray 1975). Independent boards, in contrast, are more likely to believe that only through a committee system can a large board that seldom meets get its work done (Fisher 1969).

The executive committee

Differences in boards' sizes and meeting schedules also help explain the near ubiquity of executive committees in independent institutions and their relative scarcity in the public sector; 89 percent of independent boards have executive committees, compared with 46 percent in the public sector (Taylor 1987). The executive committee is typically comprised of the board's officers and standing committee chairs and is usually authorized to act between board meetings on behalf of the full board. In general, it is prohibited only from making decisions inconsistent with prior board actions or specifically reserved for the full board, such as awarding degrees, amending bylaws, or appointing a president (Association of Governing Boards 1981).

It is suggested that the executive committee be chaired by the board chair and that it not meet more frequently than the board itself. It should be charged to act on matters that cannot wait for consideration by the full board, those issues referred to it by the full board for study, those issues the committee itself generates, and those inconsequential or pro forma matters that would consume too much scarce board time (Ingram 1985).

At its best, the executive committee is said to oversee the board's effectiveness, provide a sounding board for the president, and monitor the chief executive's morale and welfare (Ingram 1985, pp. 8–13). But the executive committee has "greater potential for good or harm" than any other committee because it is the only one "vested with the broad authority . . . held by the board itself" (p. 2).

Executive committees often do act as "inner boards" whose decisions are then ratified as a formality by the full board (Kramer 1981; Rauh 1969; Zwingle 1985). One veteran university president observes that such executive committees "have essentially taken over in such a way as to make the rest of the trustees either angry or disinterested" (quoted in Zwingle 1985, p. 17).

Differences in meeting schedules between executive committees of public and independent boards suggest that the latter are better positioned to act as "a board within a board." The executive committee meets more frequently than the board does (five times per year versus four), and 62 percent of the committee's meetings occur at regular intervals between board meetings rather than just before board meetings or on an ad hoc basis. This schedule contrasts with the pattern of most other independent and public board committees, most of which are more likely to meet just before rather than between board meetings (Taylor 1987). The implication of this schedule is that the committees' work is tied to the board's agenda and that these committees screen matters for the board's later attention rather than act as independent governing bodies.

In contrast, the executive committee in many independent institutions appears to have a formal life of its own, apart from board meetings, and to assume responsibilities that are routinized rather than ad hoc or exceptional. Contrast this with the public sector executive committee, which is found in fewer than half of the boards and which meets only twice per year on average and then most often on an ad hoc basis (Taylor 1987).

Finally, the formal life of executive committees in independent institutions is illustrated by their keeping and sharing minutes. Eighty-four percent of independent boards with executive committees keep minutes of their meetings and share them with the full board. Contrast this fact with the finding that just 59 percent of other independent board committees keep and share their minutes. In the public sector, 62 percent of both executive and other committees keep and share their minutes with the full board (Taylor 1987). One might reasonably conclude that the need to keep and share minutes reflects the extent to which the committee takes actions rather than merely studies issues and makes recommendations. Whether in the case of executive committees these matters are significant actions that arguably should be decided by the full board or instead are pro forma matters legitimately the province of the committee is not known.

Criticisms of committee structures
Critics of board committees usually object to their current structure rather than question the value of committees per se. For example, when committees on finance, investment, fund raising, and buildings and grounds work largely on administrative matters and do so in isolation from one another, how can the board develop a comprehensive financial strategy? When so many committees exist that trustees' time is spread too thinly across too many, how can the committees perform effectively? And when the structure and lines of authority become so com-

plex, at what point does the organization begin to serve its structure rather than vice versa? (O'Connell 1985; Pray 1974; Zwingle 1985).

A remedy frequently suggested is that the board should do away with many of its standing committees and appoint special ad hoc committees to deal with issues as they arise (Ruml and Morrison 1959; Zwingle 1985). Such committees would include trustees and others with special interests or expertise and would address broader, long-range policy matters rather than the administrative details usually considered by standing committees (Wood 1984a).

Board Meetings
Frequency and attendance
As we have seen, public boards meet more than twice as often as the boards of independent institutions. In addition, an inverse relationship exists between frequency and length of board meetings; while the monthly meeting of a community college board may last a few hours, the quarterly meeting of an independent college board is likely to consume one or two full days. The greatest total annual meeting time is probably seen at four-year public institutions, whose boards gather an average of nine times per year for meetings nearly as long as those characteristic of independent institutions (Nason 1982; Taylor 1987).

Some observers suggest that the board that meets infrequently (four or fewer times per year) will have difficulty fulfilling its proper role and may delegate too much authority to committees or administrators (Gould 1973; Ingram 1980a). At the same time, it is apparent that many boards that meet frequently devote their time to the wrong tasks: pro forma actions and administrative tasks (Ingram 1980a; Pray 1975).

Despite the greater frequency of board meetings in the public sector, presidents of public institutions report that, on average, 88 percent of their trustees attend each board meeting. The corresponding figure for independent boards is 78 percent. Within each sector, these figures are highly consistent across all types of institutions (Taylor 1987). Attendance rates appear to have improved in recent years. A 1974 study that asked presidents to describe board members' attendance found that between 29 and 75 percent of respondents judged their boards' attendance as "excellent." Moreover, variation between sectors and among types of institutions was great; for example, the "excellent" rating for state college boards was just 36 percent, compared with 67 percent for public universities (Davis and Batchelor 1974, p. 22).

Content and quality of board meetings
Board meetings are frequently characterized as dull affairs where passive trustees trudge through stereotyped agendas (Ingram 1980a; Nason 1982; Zwingle 1985). The agenda usually covers three kinds of material: the approval of actions taken by the executive committee and/or the administration, reports from administrators and board committees, and the authorization of new actions suggested by committees and administrators (Zwingle 1985, p. 20). Such agendas tend to be so crowded that there is usually little time or opportunity for serious discussion or participation by individual trustees (Lee and Bowen 1971; Nason 1982).

An alternative to the agenda filled with routine items, albeit an undesirable one, is the practice of some presidents of presenting to the board for immediate action an issue of major importance to the institution. Trustees will not have had background information to study nor typically will they have been given alternatives to consider. The recommendation presented in this fashion can take on the features of a vote of confidence in the president, and so the board's choice is to approve the recommendation or risk appearing to disapprove of its chief executive (Nason 1982; Nelson 1979).

A longtime board chair outlines four steps to improve board meetings:

1. Consider the most important items at the beginning of the meeting when trustees' level of interest and attention is highest.
2. Include on the agenda at least once a year a major issue that is likely to need future attention. The discussion itself will be educational for the board and the administration, and the board will not be caught by surprise when the issue surfaces later.
3. When recommendations are presented to the board for action, the alternatives should be described and the best arguments for each given. It is not sufficient for trustees to know about and discuss only the recommendation of the president.
4. Make certain that each item on the agenda is necessary and that it receives only as much of the board's time as it

requires. A routine matter should not consume as much time as an item of greater significance (Nelson 1979).

Meetings are more interesting, involving, and productive if attention is paid to varying their format and physical arrangements. Each meeting, for example, should include some special report or presentation that transcends the day's agenda and informs the board about the institution's work (O'Connell 1985; Zwingle 1980a). At one institution, one board meeting each year is devoted to reviewing the year's work and to adopting goals for the following year (Holderman 1981).

Many multicampus boards rotate meetings among their campuses to develop or enhance relationships with individual units and their personnel. The possible disadvantages of this practice include the time and expense of travel, inadequate meeting facilities on the campuses, distance from immediate access to information maintained by the central staff, and demands placed on campus administrators who must prepare for meetings (Lee and Bowen 1971, p. 128). Single-campus boards may also occasionally vary their meeting sites and schedules to prevent boredom's setting in (Ingram 1980a; O'Connell 1985; Rauh 1969).

Boards should review periodically the quality of their meetings by comparing minutes of past meetings with Nelson's four standards described earlier. A board might also try periodically ending meetings by asking trustees how they felt about the meeting, what could have been done to make it more successful, and what should be done to improve the next one (Ingram 1980a, pp. 78, 81).

Planning the agenda
Effective meetings require planning, and critics of extant board meetings often suggest that agendas be outlined a year or so in advance to allow for adequate preparation and to ensure that items requiring only periodic consideration are not overlooked (Whitehead 1985; Zwingle 1985). Planning the agenda can help boards focus on the right issues at the appropriate level. Quite simply, when trustees are not prepared to address larger issues, they are inclined to focus on minor matters (Nelson 1979). This observation may provide at least a partial explanation for the finding that most boards engage more in detailed decision mak-

ing than in the promulgation of broad policy (Paltridge, Hurst, and Morgan 1973).

The process of planning the agenda also enables trustees and others to suggest items for the board's consideration (Nason 1982). It has even been observed that boards could be enlightened by asking faculty and students to list the three topics they would most like to have the board consider (Rauh 1969).

In any case, when agendas are assembled at the last minute, the chair and the president may do so largely unassisted. And while these individuals should have primary responsibility for planning the board's work, the interest and talents of others are likely to be sacrificed if they do not feel part of the process of planning (Nason 1982; Zwingle 1985).

Minutes of board meetings must be taken carefully and kept permanently to provide a legal record of the board's actions and to serve as a "group memory" for future meetings. The minutes should be reviewed for accuracy and readability by the board chair, the president, and the professional board secretary, where one exists. Lists of attendees and those absent from the meeting included in the minutes help to "focus attention on those who frequently miss meetings" (Ingram 1980a, pp. 82–83).

Advisory Boards

Many institutions have advisory boards or committees, "voluntary, extralegal group[s] of advisors and/or supporters drawn together to give aid . . . to an educational institution or one of its subunits . . ." Cunninggim 1985, p. 1). Such groups are found in 62 percent of public institutions and 58 percent of independent colleges and universities (Taylor 1987).

Frequently, such committees provide advice or assistance with public relations or fund raising for a particular academic program or school. In other cases, and of particular interest here, local advisory boards work with and promote the interests of individual campuses in a multicampus system (Lee and Bowen 1971). Such boards are viewed as at least a partial response to the dilemma of large systems whose governing boards are perceived as distant from the needs of individual campuses. In theory, the local board provides an interested lay presence on the campus, while the governing board concerns itself with the needs of the system as a whole (Commission on Strengthening 1984; Lee and Bowen 1971).

Local boards have varying degrees of authority in the governance of systems, and their effectiveness appears to relate to the extent of their authority and the support they receive from administrators and the governing board (Cunninggim 1985).

In situations where the local board's formal authority is highly circumscribed or nonexistent, campus executives frequently view the group as a burden rather than as an asset. The executive must devote considerable time to organizing the local board's work and to devising agendas that at least appear to be meaningful, all the while working with the system office and governing board that retain real authority over the campus (Kauffman 1980). For this reason, local boards should be given final authority over as many campus concerns as possible (Clark Kerr, in the foreword to Lee and Bowen 1971).

As an alternative or adjunct to local boards, some governing boards organize the structure of their standing committees with campus relations in mind. Some have a committee for each campus in the system. The committee interacts with the campus executive and takes particular interest in the affairs of that campus. Other governing boards with conventional committee systems, rather than limiting their contact to administrators of the system's office, work directly with campus executives on matters of special concern to their campuses. These structures do not appear to undermine the authority of the system's office, which receives meeting agendas and sends representatives to committee meetings (Lee and Bowen 1971).

Assessing the Board's Performance
Assuming that they act in accordance with law, boards are formally accountable to themselves alone, exacerbating the problem of ensuring the board's effectiveness because it requires a willingness by trustees to critique themselves, something most are reluctant to do (Zwingle 1985).

Yet colleges and universities depend on their environments for financial and other forms of support. Intransigence in the face of public opinion risks loss of support for the institution and loss of confidence in the board. As discussed later, skillful administrators can sometimes find means of working around an unresponsive board by carefully selecting information, controlling the board's agenda, building a coalition with other constituents, and so on. Faculty can unionize, undermine the board's decisions through selective execution, and otherwise decline to be cooperative. In fact, many persons and groups hold boards accountable in informal ways, and boards are thus advised to adopt performance guidelines of their own "or expect to be continually on the defensive, meeting each skirmish by improvisation or reliance on available financial or political power" (Zwingle and Mayville 1974, p. 18).

It is argued that a fundamental requirement of trustees' accountability is disclosure of personal assets and potential conflicts of interest (Brewster 1971). A board cannot govern an institution responsibly if its members have personal dealings that run counter to those of the institution. This advice notwithstanding, fewer than half of the boards of colleges and universities have adopted statements regarding conflicts of interest. Moreover, in the public sector, fewer than half of the boards require disclosure of trustees' assets; among boards of independent institutions just 10 percent require disclosure (Taylor 1987).

With respect to the evaluation of the board's performance per se, the matter is complicated by the assertion that no single standard can be applied to judge the board's performance. Criteria for assessment depend on the values and expectations of the institution's creators and current constituents (Paltridge 1980), and they probably also relate in indeterminate ways to questions of administrative and educational effectiveness (Zwingle and Mayville 1974).

Nevertheless, some observers have offered lists of criteria for a board's effectiveness, most of which parallel familiar lists of the board's responsibilities. They encourage boards to assess, for example, the quality and appropriateness of their oversight of institutional mission and planning, educational policy, physical plant, and financial resources, and to evaluate the state of board membership and relations with various groups of constituents (Paltridge 1980).

Less common than criteria based on responsibility are considerations of the state of the board's internal operations. One such list encourages boards to assess, for example, attendance, quality of meetings and participation, locus of decision making (board, "inner board," or administration), quality of leadership, and the functioning of committees (Ingram 1980a).

In addition to assessments of the board, individual trustees are occasionally advised to evaluate their personal performance with respect to their knowledge of higher education and the institution, the quality of their participation in meetings, and the skills they bring to their boards (Ingram 1980c).

Assessments of the board can be conducted by trustees in meetings or by questionnaires and checklists or by outsiders. Regular board meetings can include discussions of the board's performance, though more highly recommended is the use of a special retreat for trustees whose purpose is to assess some aspect of the board's performance (Ingram 1984; Paltridge 1980). When isolated problems exist, confidential meetings between the chair and individual trustees or small groups of trustees intended to remedy the situation are sometimes called for (Paltridge 1980).

Questionnaires that ask each trustee to assess confidentially the board's performance can be aggregated to provide a composite description useful in itself or be employed as a basis for a retreat. Checklists that ask trustees to assess their personal knowledge and performance can be retained by the individual trustee or combined to provide a profile of the group (Paltridge 1980).

The use of outside facilitators for board self-studies is widely accepted. Normally, facilitators help plan the self-study's goals and processes and assist in carrying out the self-study itself, but much of the responsibility for the activity remains with the board and chief executive (Ingram 1984; Paltridge 1980). In contrast, boards may retain outside consultants who, with some advice from trustees and presidents, actually plan and carry out the assessment. This approach may be useful for boards whose membership is divided or that have difficulty diagnosing their problems and performance (Paltridge 1980).

Assessments of the board that involve institutional constituents other than the president are seen very rarely. Most boards wish to keep the process of assessment private, and in the few cases where the opinions of others are sought, they are usually gathered through confidential interviews rather than questionnaires or other public methods (Paltridge 1980).

In the absence of crisis, relatively few boards seem motivated to assess their performance. It is said that the only reasonable hope for changing this situation lies in the willingness of a few institutions to set an example for others by calling for "periodic, outside appraisal, with the result made a part of the record" (Zwingle and Mayville 1974, p. 26). In fact, a few boards have established standing committees responsible for the periodic review of the board's effectiveness (Pray 1974), but years after the practice was first recommended in the literature, both the committee and the periodic review itself are seen infrequently. At least one expert believes, however, that this situation may be changing. The Association of Governing Boards of Universities and Colleges, which assists boards in conducting self-studies, has noted increased interest by member boards in recent years in the association's self-study service.*

Summary

All boards have officers and most have standing committees in which much of the board's work is undertaken. Committee structures tend to resemble the institution's administrative organization, a circumstance that may encourage trustees' greater involvement in operational matters than in policy making.

The executive committee, normally comprised of the board's officers and standing committee chairs, may act between meetings on behalf of the board. The executive committee often performs useful functions, but in some cases it may act as a "board within a board," reducing the governing board to little more than a rubber stamp.

Board meetings require careful preparation and skillful agenda planning to be interesting and effective. A variety of suggestions have been offered for developing workable agendas, encouraging trustees' enthusiastic participation in meetings, and ensuring that the institution's most essential business is carried out expeditiously.

Some multicampus systems appoint advisory boards that work with individual units of the institution. Such boards are intended to provide an interested lay presence on the campus, though their effectiveness appears to vary with the extent of their authority and the support administrators and trustees provide to them.

Most boards are formally accountable to themselves alone. Despite suggestions in the literature that they assess their own performance, few seem willing to do so. Some recent anecdotal evidence suggests, however, that boards' interest in self-assessment may be increasing.

*Richard T. Ingram 1987, personal communication.

SHARING AUTHORITY WITH TRUSTEES

A statement by the American Association of University Professors, the American Council on Education, and the Association of Governing Boards of Universities and Colleges claims:

> *The variety and complexity of the tasks performed by institutions of higher education produce an inescapable interdependence among governing boards, administrators, faculty, students, and others. The relationship calls for adequate communication among these components and full opportunity for appropriate joint planning and effort* (AAUP 1966, p. 375).

The notion outlined in the statement that boards must share with others responsibility for such crucial matters as planning, budgeting, selecting senior administrators, and speaking on behalf of the institution is a logical outgrowth of observations concerning the nature of authority in colleges and universities. "Formal authority is based on legitimacy (or generalized deference to authority) and position, whereas functional authority is based on competence and person" (Mortimer and McConnell 1978, p. 19). Trustees rely mainly on formal authority, while administrators and faculty members seeking to influence boards do so largely through the exercise of functional authority.

The problem inherent in efforts to reconcile these two forms of authority is that "tension exists between those who have formal authority and those who acknowledge only functional authority" (Mortimer and McConnell 1978, p. 23). The "intellectual vitality" of colleges and universities depends on allowing considerable autonomy to academic experts, but at the same time, a complex academic institution cannot be managed without some reliance on formal authority (p. 23). In fact, as discussed earlier, boards share considerable authority with institutional constituents, including presidents, other administrators, and faculty members. Groups generally claim certain "spheres of influence" (Baldridge, Curtis, and Riley 1978, p. 71), which appear to correspond to tradition and expertise.

Results of a survey of faculty and administrators at 249 colleges and universities illustrate this phenomenon clearly (Baldridge, Curtis, and Riley 1978, p. 72). Faculty are most influential in developing curricula, while the influence of presidents and trustees is more apparent in "global" matters and long-range planning (see table 4).

Similarly, a 1982 survey of decision making in public higher

Trustees rely mainly on formal authority, while administrators and faculty members seeking to influence boards do so largely through the exercise of functional authority.

TABLE 4

"SPHERES OF INFLUENCE" RATINGS OF CERTAIN PEOPLE AND GROUPS OVER DIFFERENT ISSUES

	Developing Curricula	Appointing Faculty	Selecting Department Heads	Long-Range Palanning	"Global" or General Influence
Department faculty and committees	4.2	2.8	3.1	2.5	2.2
Department heads	3.9	3.9	2.4	3.0	2.6
Collegewide faculty committees	3.1	2.3	1.8	3.5	3.5
Deans	3.2	4.1	3.8	3.8	3.6
President and staff	2.1	2.2	2.6	4.5	3.7
Trustees	1.2	1.4	1.2	4.0	3.1

Note: On a scale of 1 to 5, 1 is low and 5 is high.

Source: Baldridge, Curtis, and Riley 1978, p. 72.

education, directed to 200 chief executives of university systems, two- and four-year institutions, and higher education agencies, revealed extensive agreement among respondents regarding the authority exercised by various groups over each of 39 academic decisions. For example, most agreed that governing boards define campus missions and objectives, campus administrators establish minimum faculty-student contact hours, and faculty at the department level determine course content and objectives (Carnegie Foundation 1982, pp. 96–113).

Relationships between the Board and Administrators
The board and the president
The effective relationship between board and president is frequently described as a harmonious partnership based on mutual support and trust. Yet the relationship is paradoxical. The board is vested with final authority over institutional policies and practices and is authorized to hire and dismiss the president. At the same time, the board depends on the president for information and for the development and execution of policy (Middleton 1983; Odendahl and Boris 1983; Senor 1963; Taylor 1984b).

In addition to conflicting roles, several studies suggest that board members and institutional executives hold opposing values and perceptions of organizational goals, which might also be expected to encourage conflict between boards and presidents (Hartnett 1969; Kramer 1965).

Presidents now serve an average of seven years in a given position, down significantly from the 10- to 14-year terms seen earlier in this century (Cohen and March 1974, p. 162; Kerr and Gade 1986, p. 22). Most incoming presidents expect to serve longer than they do, but many resign, citing problems with their governing boards as a motivating factor. Between 1971 and 1981, "relationship with the governing board" rose from number 14 to number 3 in a list of reasons most frequently offered by former presidents explaining why they had resigned (Alton 1982, p. 48). Incumbent presidents also report feeling alienated from their boards and vulnerable to the exercise of trustees' power. One lamented, "All they have to do is whisper and I'm gone" (Wood 1984a, p. 42).

But to accept that the board-president relationship is in some respects contradictory is not tantamount to believing that it is inherently dysfunctional. To the contrary, it is an "exchange relationship" in which the board and president depend on each other and tend to maintain a balance of power to derive certain desired benefits; the president receives needed "sanction and support" from trustees, while board members "gain prestige and validation of their positions as community leaders" (Kramer 1965, p. 113).

In addition, authority is exchanged. The functional authority the president possesses by virtue of expertise is exchanged for the formal authority trustees are accorded in institutional charters. Neither form of authority is sufficient without the other, and thus the mutuality of the board-president relationship is reinforced.

The process of selecting trustees, particularly in independent institutions, also tends to maintain and reinforce the balance of power between board and president. New members probably resemble the incumbents who selected the president, and, to the extent that presidents can influence the selection and education of trustees, they are likely to help maintain boards that support them. Moreover, over time, board members exposed to the institution and its norms tend to reflect the values of professionals in the organization, even if those values differ from those associated with the trustee's personal and professional value system (Kramer 1965). This process of cooptation also contributes to harmony between board and president.

In addition, as we have seen, most institutional issues have low salience for most board members. Trustees, particularly of high-status institutions, seek personal satisfaction from their board memberships and tend to be conflict averse, in turn resulting in an inclination to compromise and a desire to share authority with the president.

Perhaps it is because of the nature of the board-president exchange relationship that considerable evidence suggests agreement between trustees and presidents on such matters as the roles of board and president, the importance of various academic issues, and perceptions of the board's effectiveness and its correlates. A study of 234 presidents and board chairs, in fact, revealed striking consensus about the importance of 20 possible presidential roles (Cote 1985).

In another study, 549 presidents and trustees surveyed were found to agree nearly completely about their perceptions of their boards' involvement in 31 possible areas of academic decision making. Furthermore, the study revealed strong agreement between presidents and trustees regarding the importance to their institutions of various academic issues. Finally, board members reported a high level of reliance on and confidence in the information presidents provide to enlighten the board's decisions in academic matters (Taylor 1984b).

A third study, which examined trustees' and presidents' perceptions of the board's effectiveness, demonstrates concurrence on several factors associated with perceptions of effectiveness. The study also demonstrates considerable consistency between trustees' and presidents' opinions regarding such issues as the changes needed to improve the board's functioning, the influence of selected factors on the board's decision making (the president's recommendations are seen as most crucial), factors that hamper the board's functioning, and the value ascribed to various kinds of information provided to trustees (Davis and Batchelor 1974). Moreover, 74 percent of presidents surveyed described board members as "very helpful" in "providing personal support and sustaining friendship" (p. 33).

Guidelines for the president

Despite the acknowledged centrality of the board-president relationship and sporadic evidence that trustees and presidents agree on many issues, the relationship remains imperfectly understood and resists efforts to "reduce [it] to concrete guidelines that apply to specific cases" (Wood 1984a, p. 38). Nevertheless, by bearing in mind the features of the exchange relationship, it is possible to posit some general rules to guide presidents in their dealings with boards.

Most important, presidents are advised that boards cannot do their work without the assistance of the president (Kauffman 1980; Millett 1980a; Rauh 1973). Characteristically, this assistance includes the responsibilities to educate, inform, and motivate the board. In controlling these processes, the president assumes a powerful position vis-à-vis a board that technically occupies a superior position. In fact, the president becomes the acknowledged leader of many boards whose members look to the chief executive for ideas, recommended actions, and information about the board's appropriate behavior (Kauffman 1980; Lewis 1980; Odendahl and Boris 1983; Wood 1985).

Information and communication. A study of time presidents spend with members of various constituencies reveals that presidents spend 8 percent of their time with trustees and that contacts are as likely to be initiated by the president as by a trustee (Cohen and March 1974, pp. 130, 136). In a more recent

study, presidents report spending 25 percent of their time on board-related activities, which would include preparation for meetings, cultivation of prospective board members, and so on (Wood 1985, p. 61).

Apparently presidents believe that contact with trustees is important to sound board-president relations, but many chief executives are hard pressed to devote as much time to the effort as they feel is needed (Wood 1984a). The results of this neglect are apparent. Thirty-five percent of trustees surveyed in a 1974 study indicated that the president's failure to communicate effectively with the board hampered the board's work to a moderate or considerable extent—an opinion shared, interestingly, by 31 percent of the presidents surveyed (Davis and Batchelor 1974, p. 29).

The failure to give sufficient attention represents missed opportunities to improve current board-president relations and to build the mutual trust needed to see the president through future difficulties with the board or institution. The chief executive who distances the board from the life of the institution and who fails to keep trustees fully informed is likely to see the board act inappropriately (Ingram 1980b; Millett 1980a).

Informal communication is as important as formal contact. Trustees should feel they have ready access to the president (Holderman 1981), and the president should seek one-to-one contact with board members, socialize with them, and do "uncompromising" personal favors for trustees (Fisher 1984, p. 159). Such contacts enable the president to test ideas before raising them formally and also provide useful information about public opinion (Gould 1973; Holderman 1981; Wood 1985). The president is advised, however, to avoid informal counsel with trustees that is tantamount to formal action; the legal governance structure should not be undermined by informal contact (Rauh 1969).

The matter of what and how much to communicate with the board is disputed. The advice most frequently given to presidents is to share all information the board needs to govern intelligently—both good and bad news (Commission on Strengthening 1984; Rauh 1969).

In general, the more complex the institution and its operations, the more readily the president can control the information the board receives (Kramer 1965; Senor 1963). And because some presuppose that trustees who know a great deal will interfere accordingly in administrative matters, the temptation to be less than candid can be substantial. One president whose board tends mostly to matters of finance and physical plant describes himself as a "translator" with respect to academic issues. "A less tactful but more accurate analogy might liken the president to a guardian who protects the curriculum from any potential incursions by the governing board" (Wood 1984a, p. 40).

The costs to the president who misjudges the board's expectations for information can be high, however. Far from preventing interference, the absence of candor may cause it. That is, once the board is caught by surprise, trustees will wonder what else has been kept from them and will begin to interfere inappropriately (Meardy 1977). Quite simply, "unless a board is confident that the president is informing them of the significant issues confronting the institution, enlightened board members will seek such information elsewhere" (Kauffman 1980, p. 61).

Agendas and meetings. The president assumes primary responsibility for developing agendas for board meetings and for providing background material to support them (Corson 1980; Holderman 1981). Planning agendas should be a long-term, continuing process in which a coherent view of the institution's goals and priorities guides the selection and timing of issues for the board's consideration. Issues should be raised early enough that trustees' comments and suggestions can be incorporated into the work that precedes formal consideration by the board (Dorsey 1980; Gould 1973; Ruml and Morrison 1959). A proposal for a new academic program, for example, should not be presented for the first time to the board as a finished product whose acceptance or rejection then becomes the equivalent of a vote of confidence in the president. Rather, trustees should be involved at the start of the program-planning process, in approving the development of the program and in establishing the objectives it is intended to serve. Trustees should also receive periodic progress reports as development continues (Chait 1984).

Annual board agendas might arise from an "annual memorandum on academic strategy" prepared by the president and senior administrators that

> . . . raises questions, highlights problems, and suggests future directions . . . in which the [president] wishes to guide the faculty and the institution . . . . The content of the mem-

*orandum should answer the question: "What is your vision
for this institution and how do you expect to achieve it?"*
(Wood 1984b, pp. 19–20).

Background material provided to trustees to support board
agendas is frequently criticized as unsuitable in depth, breadth,
or format to the needs of trustees, because it usually stems
from reporting systems developed to support administrative
rather than governance decisions (Chait and Taylor 1983; Pocock 1980). Moreover, sophisticated information systems enable administrators to produce "mountains of data" (Baldridge,
Curtis, and Riley 1978, p. 214), which overwhelm trustees and
are often next to useless for informing specific decisions
(Gould 1973; Pray 1975; Wessell 1974).

A suggested remedy is a schedule of information to be provided to the board that parallels the board's long-term agenda.
If the board plans, for example, to review the institution's policies regarding tenure, it may request months in advance information on staffing plans, tenure levels, turnover rates,
allocation of resources, student demand, and so forth. Such information can be provided in a form and at a level of aggrega-
tion that encourages attention to broad tenure policy rather than
invites board members to second-guess individual recommendations for tenure (Chait and Taylor 1983).

Once decisions are made, presidents are advised to provide
regular progress reports to trustees regarding the execution of
those decisions. This practice can provide the board with a
sense of accomplishment, reinforce their commitment to their
decisions and to the president carrying them out, and help prevent the board's taking actions that unwittingly undermine previous decisions (Radock and Jacobson 1980; Zwingle 1985).

Where open-meeting laws do not prohibit them, executive
sessions in which the president—with or without senior administrators—meets privately with the board at the end of a board
meeting provide an opportunity for all to speak frankly about
concerns before they erupt as serious problems. Conducted regularly, such sessions promote cohesiveness and trust between
the board and the president. "The confident president . . .
should not hesitate to propose the idea" (Ingram 1980a, p. 80;
see also Kauffman 1980).

Contacts with others. As we have seen, the principal and
most trusted sources of information for most boards are the

president and the president's senior staff (Corson 1975; Green-leaf 1974; Taylor 1984b). Whether or not boards and presidents are well served by this arrangement, however, is a matter of some dispute.

One former president is particularly opposed to contact between the board and anyone but the president, believing that presidential power is eroded if access to the board is shared. He suggests that faculty and students not be allowed to attend or participate in board meetings and that they not be members of board committees. Moreover, he argues, no administrator but the president should attend executive sessions of the board. If the president is the board's sole window on the institution, and vice versa, the president's "mystique" and "charisma" will be maintained and his or her influence with both board and institution enhanced (Fisher 1984, pp. 163–71).

Another president's concern about the board's contact with faculty and students is more mundane. He reportedly objects to such communication because it tends to encourage trustees' involvement in purely operational matters (Wood 1985). Others suggest, however, that in the absence of such contact, trustees cannot be well enough informed to govern effectively (Corson 1975). If the board must rely solely on the president and senior administrators for information, "there is an upward filtering . . . through which much of the essence of the problem may be lost" (Rauh 1969, p. 20).

Believing that boards should not be secluded and that as a practical matter most cannot be, some observers suggest encouraging open but structured communication between trustees and campus constituents arranged with the knowledge and approval of, and sometimes with the participation of, the president and senior administrators. Meetings, seminars, retreats, and social events can encourage open communication that may obviate the need for private contact between trustees and constituents (Chait and Taylor 1983; Odendahl and Boris 1983). As a participant in this process of communication, the president retains the roles of educator of the board and possessor of functional authority that are crucial to maintaining the exchange relationship with the board.

Motivating the board. A corollary to the president's responsibility to educate and inform the board is the obligation to motivate trustees' continuing interest in the board's and the institution's affairs. "The interested trustee is the informed trustee and the worked trustee'' (Bean 1975, p. 40). Each board member should be oriented to trusteeship and to the institution and should have a specific responsibility based on his or her particular talents and interests (Whitehead 1985). Presidents can do much to improve the quality of board meetings and thus to encourage trustees' enthusiastic and productive involvement. And, as we have seen, altruism motivates trustees to some degree, but so also does public recognition. Thanks expressed to trustees and spouses, awards given where appropriate, and other acts that convey appreciation can help keep trustees involved and committed (Pray 1974).

Effective boards are involved with the institution, informed about its affairs, and have a corporate sense of purpose that transcends trustees' individual viewpoints (Chaffee 1984; Nason 1982). Creating and maintaining this collective intent is made difficult by certain individual and group characteristics that tend to divide the board.

First, it has been observed of the voting population that approximately 10 percent are ''activists'' whom the rest of the electorate allow to rule with little interference or consultation. ''Spectators,'' accounting for some 60 percent of the population, enter the fray during periods of crisis and restrain the activists' freedom of action. The remaining 30 percent of the electorate—the ''apathetics''—seldom participate at all (McConnell 1971, p. 102).

This observation applies as well to boards of trustees whose work and values are determined in large part by the president, chair, committee chairs, and other active members (Wood 1985). The president who reinforces this state of affairs by dealing only with the powerful minority may forgo the potential contributions of the majority and with that their interest in the board, the institution, and the president himself or herself.

Related factors of individual expertise, social status, philosophy, and personality may divide boards and cause difficulty for presidents. Board members and presidents bring individual resources to the governance of institutions—skills, personal characteristics, connections to the environment, money, and so on (Zald 1969). The balance of power that characterizes the exchange relationship will be upset in situations where any of the parties possess more significant resources than the others, are willing to use them, and are deferred to because of them. Under such conditions, the trustee who is a major donor, politically connected, financially astute, or captive to a personal cause may come to exercise far more influence than other board members or the president (see, for example, Kauffman 1977; Wood 1985; Zwingle 1981).

Such divisions within the board can lead to disputes and power struggles between trustees. The president who becomes involved in these difficulties will invariably suffer for failing to please someone (Fisher 1984; Kauffman 1980). And to the extent that the president has failed to interest, educate, and involve less active trustees in the board's work, potential allies will have been lost.

Influencing the selection and development of trustees. Most presidents work to influence the process of selecting trustees to the extent that the method of selection allows. When the president succeeds in this endeavor, he or she will have helped to shape a board that will provide personal support and backing for presidential initiatives (Epstein 1974).

In public institutions where trustees are politically appointed, informal contact between the president, the board chair, and the governor and/or legislators may aid in the selection of trustees acceptable to the president and the board (Rauh 1969). While the efficacy of this influence is constrained in situations where the president and incumbent trustees are heavily identified with previous office holders, "more or less desirable choices always occur within the party whose opportunity is at hand" (Epstein 1974, p. 82). At the very least, presidents, with the support of trustees, can seek to minimize the potential threat associated with new appointments.

Presidents of independent institutions are in a stronger position to influence the selection of trustees. Presumably they have the confidence of the board members who appointed and retain them—the same board members who are charged with making most appointments of trustees (Epstein 1974). In fact, the president's role in recruiting trustees at most independent institutions is so "deeply entrenched" that, for example, one board chair reportedly "fears that a stronger trustee presence in recruitment might offend the president" (Wood 1985, p. 82).

It is the president, after all, who is probably more willing than most trustees to give time to the cultivation of prospective board members because no one has more to gain from attracting the right trustees. This investment of effort can result in the appointment of board members who are simultaneously knowledgeable about the trustee's role as the president views it, com-

Effective boards are involved with the institution, informed about its affairs, and have a corporate sense of purpose that transcends trustees' individual viewpoint.

mitted to the institution, and loyal to the person most responsible for their recruitment—the president. And, in addition to these benefits, some chief executives view their involvement in the process as an offensive maneuver intended to upgrade the board's quality. Given the tendency of self-perpetuating boards to select members who resemble themselves, a selection process controlled solely by the board is likely to beget boards no better than their predecessors (Wood 1985).

The orientation of new trustees and the continuing education of incumbents are considered primarily presidential responsibilities shared with the nominating or some comparable board committee. The president is advised to guide the committee as it plans development activities for trustees and then to take the lead in implementing the programs (Ingram 1984).

Formal orientation programs, provided by approximately 60 percent of colleges and universities (Taylor 1987), should include activities like campus tours; presentations on institutional characteristics, strengths, and weaknesses; time to interact informally with faculty, administrators, and students; and some opportunity for the individual trustee to be briefed about a matter of particular personal interest, to visit a class, or to offer a guest lecture. In addition, descriptive information about the institution, board members, and key administrators, faculty, and students should be provided. Often neglected in such programs is orientation to trusteeship itself, which should concern the board's role and the role of individual trustees (Ingram 1984; Nason 1982; Rauh 1973).

Boards are advised to provide for occasional workshops or retreats to consider major problems and emerging issues that are beyond the scope of the agendas of normal meetings. These programs can consider such matters as assessing the board's organization and performance, discussing the institution's planning process or recommendations, or considering the major environmental factors likely to affect the institution in the future (Baldridge, Curtis, and Riley 1978; Ingram 1984; Keller 1983; Nason 1982; Savage 1982).

Presidents seeking to influence the board's thinking and behavior are well advised to take their role in orientation and development programs seriously. To the extent that the president's position as the board's educator is accepted and reinforced, the exchange relationship that empowers the president will be strengthened (Kramer 1965).

Relationships with others. The president's position vis-à-vis the board can be enhanced or harmed by the character of his or her nonboard relationships. A president supported by faculty, staff, donors, educational leaders, and the public is likely to have the respect of the board as well, because trustees learn about the president from others, not from the president, "whose energies will be better spent building a base of support" outside the boardroom (Fisher 1984, p. 157).

Fisher, who thinks little of the quality of most multicampus public boards, adds that the president who deals obsequiously with such a board will "seem inept by association" and will lose the support of faculty, students, staff, and external authorities (p. 156). Put somewhat differently, the president who shows concern for all constituents will be more knowledgeable and effective in guiding the board and in executing its policy decisions (Kauffman 1980).

The president's relationship with the faculty is especially influential in defining the character of the board-president relationship. Boards, as discussed earlier, tend to be conflict averse, and so they generally support a president whose constituents, particularly the faculty, are tranquil (Wood 1985). Situations in which the faculty is in conflict with the board or president can "immobilize" the chief executive (Commission on Strengthening 1984, p. 5).

The difficulty many presidents face is that consistently good relationships with faculty are elusive. Faculty tend to resist change and are frequently in conflict among themselves and with administrators over the institution's goals and the allocation of resources (Baldridge, Curtis, and Riley 1978). The president makes decisions that are bound to be disappointing to some and over a period of time may succeed one by one in offending most of the faculty, whose collective enthusiasm for the president is likely to suffer (Ruml and Morrison 1959).

Presidential style. The president's "dedication and professional integrity are his armor, and any crack in that armor is focused on with more criticism than if found in the attitudes or actions [of trustees]" (Auerbach 1961, p. 72). The president's disposition to reason rather than rant, to tell the truth, and to resist the urge to discuss personalities and to gossip encourages the board's respect and trust (Corson 1975, 1980; Fisher 1984; Rauh 1969). As a foundation executive has observed, "If you have a lot of trust, there's really no limit to the amount of creativity that the board will allow. If you don't have it, there's just no end to the troubles of trying to do anything" (quoted in Odendahl and Boris 1983, p. 42).

Trust is not earned through timidity and self-effacement. As Theodore M. Hesburgh, long-time president of the University of Notre Dame, observed:

> There are times when a president will have to try to change trustees' minds regarding basic policy. At least he should leave no doubt about where he stands. Trustees need to be informed clearly and forcefully, on a continuing basis, regarding the institution's most basic needs. The president must resist when trustees interfere in the administration, attempting to govern rather than ensure good government. I have found that this stance is both appreciated and supported by trustees. A spirit of confidence on the part of a president begets confidence on the part of trustees. . . .
> There may even come a time when the president must say, "Here I stand." It may be the end of the relationship, but rarely is. Even trustees, or maybe especially trustees, respect integrity (quoted in Kerr and Gade 1986, p. 211).

The willingness of presidents to do their homework also enhances their relationships with boards. When the president prepares a recommendation carelessly or is not in command of related facts and data, it is easy for the board to dismiss the recommendation and begin to distrust the president. It is a short step from this contention to the frequently heard admonition that the president should never bring an idea to the board unless confident of its support (Odendahl and Boris 1983). Not only is this practice said to enhance the president's stature as the board's trusted chief executive, but it is thought also to discourage personal intervention in institutional affairs by trustees unhappy with a recommendation or uneasy about the president's leadership. Moreover, high-status, conflict-averse boards are likely to welcome efforts by the chief executive to bring "safe" recommendations to the board and thus to preempt controversy (Middleton 1983).

Another perspective on this question is provided by those who maintain that differences of opinion within boards and between boards and presidents are inevitable and even healthy.

If you are dealing with real issues, striving too hard for compromise and unity may mean that you are not facing squarely the issues themselves, you don't have the right mix of people, or you've watered down the issues until they're harmless and impotent. . . . It is far better to lose even on critical issues as long as the organization comes out of the battle with greater confidence in the integrity of the process (O'Connell 1985, pp. 30–31).

It is worth noting that O'Connell's subject is the governance of voluntary organizations in general, many of which have constituent-oriented boards. The ability of the chief executive in such cases to avoid controversy by bringing only safe issues to the board is constrained by the willingness of such boards to engage in conflict, a propensity not usually shared by high-status boards.

Presidents are sometimes advised to seek regular, formal assessment by their boards. The process, which should begin with a self-assessment by the president (Nason 1984), provides the chief executive an opportunity to correct the oversimplified view of the presidential role that many trustees maintain. It enables the president to articulate goals, highlight successes, and identify areas where the board's help is needed (Munitz 1980). It allows the president to preempt critics by pointing out faults and suggesting remedies before someone else does it. And, almost invariably, the assessment of the president extends to the board; given the interdependent nature of the relationship, it is difficult to consider one portion of it without also looking at the other (Nason 1984). Thus, to the extent that the president can control the conduct of the evaluation or the board can be trusted to manage it skillfully, its potential for benefiting rather than harming the president is increased.

Lowered expectations. The image of the board-president relationship as a partnership gives rise to assumptions of unquestioning mutual support that are probably unrealistic, given the paradoxical nature of the actual relationship. Thus, "most experienced college presidents distinguish between the 'ideal' board, which supports the president, and their own boardrooms where. . .'when things get tough, a few trustees always get bitchy'" (Wood 1985, p. 49).

Presidents are advised to accept as inevitable that some trustees will criticize no matter what the president does, some will be unmoving in the face of evidence that their position is wrong, and others will fail to read materials provided or otherwise prepare for meetings and take their responsibilities as a trustee seriously (Wessell 1974). In multicampus systems, campus presidents are counseled to expect little support or influence from distant and too often uninterested system boards (Fisher 1984).

In the face of these and similar problems, presidents are advised to be generous and patient and to maintain a sense of humor and an emotional distance that allows a dispassionate perspective (Cheit 1971; Commission on Strengthening 1984). As one president puts it, "Don't give all of your heart to the institution—if you do, you may lose it" (Commission on Strengthening 1984, p. 94).

 **Choosing wisely.** In his *Maxims for a Young College President*, Herman Wells, president for 25 years of Indiana University, exhorted the president first to "be lucky" (quoted in Commission on Strengthening 1984, p. 218). The advice of many others suggests that presidents make their own luck, primarily by understanding the institution before accepting the position, selecting a position compatible with the individual's strengths, and reaching agreements in advance with trustees regarding mutual expectations.

Two recent studies of the college and university presidency concluded that, from the perspective of the president, chances of success are greater in independent institutions whose boards are generally more effective and committed than those of public institutions. Within the public sector, larger boards are preferable to smaller ones, which can too easily be dominated by a vocal minority. And longer rather than shorter terms for trustees are desirable, as over time board members are more likely to become skillful and committed to the institution (Commission on Strengthening 1984; Kerr and Gade 1986).

Success is more readily found in working with ratifying or corporate rather than participatory boards.

> *Trustees on a ratifying board are likely to give strong support with few questions asked, those on a corporate board to give public support while asking a good many searching questions of the president privately and in the boardroom, and those on a participatory board to express openly their own personal views . . . In other words, the strength of the*

*obligation a board member feels to support a president var-
ies according to the board's operating style* (Wood 1985, p.
141).

The presidency is more manageable in an institution with a
clear sense of mission, that is located in a growing area, whose
constituents are homogeneous rather than fractionated, and
where the presidency carries prestige and respect (Commission
on Strengthening 1984; Kerr and Gade 1986). Data on presidential turnover support these generalities. Turnover is lower in
independent than in public institutions and in selective than in
less selective colleges and universities (Kerr and Gade 1986).

Approximately 80 percent of presidents are hired from outside the institution, and most of them have not served previously as presidents (David Riesman, in the introduction to Kerr
and Gade 1986). Inexperience and lack of exposure to the institution frequently lead to unpleasant surprises, many of which
involve the board. By definition, these surprises cannot easily
be predicted, but forewarned to look for them prospective presidents can become sensitive to subtle signals of likely trouble.

Surprises most frequently encountered include the nature and
intensity of the board's internal politics, including questions of
who has influence over what and what operating style the board
has adopted.

The board's attitude toward dealings with the new president's
predecessor and its posture regarding incumbent staff members
may also be unknowns. Some staff may be "untouchable,"
and insofar as possible the prospective president should try to
identify these individuals and determine whether and how he or
she can live with them (Commission on Strengthening 1984;
Kerr and Gade 1986).

Objective data about the institution's financial and nonfinancial condition should also be examined. Boards have been
known to mislead presidential candidates about the health of
the institution (Kauffman 1977).

In addition to assessing the institution, presidential candidates should consider the compatibility of specific positions
with their abilities, physical and psychological strength, family
situation, personal values, administrative style, and so on
(Commission on Strengthening 1984). The best board cannot
compensate for a poor fit between the president and the institution.

Presidential candidates should also consider and discuss in

advance with the board its expectations for performance, plans for performance reviews, responsibilities of the spouse, if any, and terms of office and exit from the position (Kerr and Gade 1986, pp. 180–81).

Exits are smoothed for presidents who serve under the terms of a written contract or who have faculty rank and tenure. Presidential contracts are found in 62 percent of public institutions versus 55 percent of independent colleges and universities. Contracts are particularly prevalent in two-year public colleges (86 percent) and among the chief executives of public multicampus and state systems (89 percent). Academic rank and tenure are also given more frequently to presidents in the public sector (39 percent) than to chief executives in the independent sector (27 percent), though just 13 percent of public two-year college presidents have academic rank and tenure (Taylor 1987). Thus, if the presidency is somewhat less stable in the public sector, the public incumbent is more likely to experience an exit smoothed by advance warning of termination, a contract buy-out, or the guarantee of a tenured faculty position to occupy.

System heads and campus executives in multicampus systems
Approximately one-half of all public campuses in the United States are units of multicampus systems, as are just 5 percent of independent campuses (Commission on Strengthening 1984, p. 71). Both systems and campuses have chief executives, and it is the balance of authority between these individuals that defines the character of the system (Pettit 1987). In some multicampus systems, campus chief executives report directly to the governing board, while in others the system executive alone reports to the board and campus heads are responsible to the system head (Lee and Bowen 1971).

Among state systems the latter pattern—that of the strong system executive—has been the more prevalent because it reduces the "reporting burden" placed on boards and enables boards to hold one executive rather than several campus heads responsible for the activities of the organization (Millett 1984, p. 136).

This pattern had led to problems for some campus executives, who have "expectations that flow from the original trusteeship model" (Kauffman 1980, p. 65). That is, they expect board members to know, visit, and support their individual campuses, but "more often than not, they are doomed to disappointment'' (p. 65). Systems have become so complex that few of their governing boards are familiar with conditions on individual campuses.

In instances where campus executives have direct access to governing boards, however, other problems frequently result. Not surprisingly, campus executives in a system usually act as individuals rather than as a group, which tends to undermine the cohesiveness and coordination that systems are created to foster (Lee and Bowen 1971). Direct access is also thought to encourage the board's involvement in campus administrative detail to the neglect of systemwide policy making (Pettit 1987).

So-called strong system executives, those who stand between campus heads and the governing board, frequently operate under conditions that undermine their ability to establish functional exchange relationships with their boards. To review, such relationships are based on the exchange of critical resources, which in the case of presidents include the support of constituents, control of data and opinions, professional expertise, and personal characteristics. As in the case of presidents of single-campus institutions, to the extent that system executives control these resources, they may be expected to occupy relatively more influential positions vis-à-vis their boards.

The support of constituents is an especially troubling issue for system executives. Unlike presidents of single-campus institutions, system executives have no constituencies of their own. Faculty, alumni, students, donors, local legislators, community citizens, and so on are likely to identify with individual campuses and to give no support to the system per se, which is an abstraction in the minds of most. Thus, the system executive "depends solely on the unremitting support of his trustees, many of whom may be alumni or in some other sense partisans of institutions that he supervises" (Pettit 1987, p. 9).

Another view holds that system executives can work to foster cordial and mutually supportive relationships with campuses (Millett 1984). These relationships might themselves be conceived as exchange relationships in which campus and system executives seek a mutually beneficial balance of power. To the extent that campus executives depend on and profit from the exchange, they may be inclined to provide support that the system executive may in turn exchange with the board.

With respect to provision of information, communication with constituents, setting of agendas, and other responsibilities that concern the flow of data and opinions to trustees, the system executive who controls these processes is likely to be in a stronger position vis-à-vis the board than the system head who shares control with others, particularly campus executives.

Campus executives, except in the largest systems, normally attend and sometimes participate in board meetings. Individual board members or committees sometimes visit campuses and interact with campus personnel. Board agendas are occasionally controlled by and in other cases substantially influenced by campus executives (Pettit 1987). Under these and similar circumstances, the functional authority of the system executive is reduced.

Finally, the system executive's professional expertise and personal qualities, to the extent that they are not outshone or eclipsed by those of campus executives, are likely to enhance the system executive–board relationship.

Obviously, the allocation of formal authority between system and campus executives bears on the nature of the relationships of each with the governing board. When the system executive has primary authority over appointments and dismissals of campus executives and other campus personnel, operating budgets, program approval, purchasing, legislative relations, and other matters of importance to campuses, the system executive's position in relation to the board will be enhanced relative to that of the campus executives (Commission on Strengthening 1984; Pettit 1987).

In addition to the caveats that apply to any prospective president, some special cautions might well be observed by the would-be system executive. Matters of consequence include the formal and functional allocation of authority between the system office and campuses and the congruence between the allocation of authority and the board's expectations of accountability (Commission on Strengthening 1984; Pettit 1987). One might also be well advised to study the style of predecessor executives, who often have had more influence on shaping the character of the position and the board's interaction with it than written policies that technically govern the allocation of authority (Kauffman 1980). The board's policy manual may assign responsibility to the system executive that has been disregarded by the executive or whose implementation is undermined by resistance from campus constituents or by irresolute support from the board. In such cases, the system executive's functional authority is likely to be circumscribed (Pettit 1987).

The board chair and the president

Nowhere in the literature on governance is the image of partnership more consistently applied than in discussions of the relationship between president and chair. The chair personifies the board's authority, and the chair-president relationship personifies the exchange of expertise and authority that enables the paradoxical board-president relationship to function.

In distinguishing the president's role from that of the chair-president team, George N. Rainsford indicates that the president manages the institution, but the president and chair together are responsible for its leadership (quoted in Pocock 1984a, p. 1). Responsibilities for joint leadership attributed to the two include ensuring the board's effectiveness, providing for profitable board meetings, and determining that fundamental institutional responsibilities are discharged.

The board's effectiveness is improved when the president and the chair act together to define the board's role, provide stimulating committee assignments, call on inactive trustees to contribute to the board's work, rotate noncontributing members off the board, if possible, and select and develop effective new trustees (Nason 1982; Nelson 1973; Pocock 1984a; Rauh 1969).

The quality of meetings is enhanced when the president and the chair jointly define crucial issues, determine priorities, identify needed information, establish desired outcomes, and plan agendas accordingly (Pocock 1984a). It is largely through the joint efforts of the president and the chair that trustees are "energized rather than bored" by meetings (Zwingle 1985, p. 22). Meetings can also be improved if the chair and the president, perhaps with key staff, go through a dry run of the agenda a day or two before the meeting to ensure that both the board's and president's expectations will be met (Pocock 1984a, p. 5) and then, after the meeting, if the president and the chair review what occurred and plan for future improvements (Ingram 1980a).

Finally, the president and the chair are jointly responsible for determining that planning, rational allocation of resources, and evaluation of the institution's activities are effectively accomplished (Pocock 1984a). These responsibilities are among the board's most fundamental and are the functions on which all other activities of the board and institution should rest. At the same time, the president's leadership role is inextricably linked

The chair personifies the board's authority, and the chair-president relationship personifies the exchange of expertise and authority that enables the paradoxical board-president relationship to function.

with each of these areas of responsibility, and so the need for joint chair-president oversight is apparent.

Senior administrators and the board

Most of the authority of senior administrators in relation to boards derives from presidential delegation. To the extent, then, that deans and vice presidents who work with boards are exercising presidential authority, much of the advice offered to presidents for improving their relationships with boards also pertains to other senior administrators. An exchange relationship, for example, may be said to exist between trustees and the deans and vice presidents who provide boards with information and who carry out their decisions. The character of formal and informal communication with trustees can serve to strengthen or hamper a dean's or vice president's position with the board. The information senior administrators provide to trustees can influence the nature and quality of the board's involvement in institutional affairs. A dean's or vice president's relationships with others, particularly the faculty and president, are likely to influence the board's perceptions of his or her effectiveness, and when respect from others is evident, the board is likely to join in that sentiment. So also do matters of personal style and wise selection of position influence the character of a senior administrator's relationship with the board.

In most institutions, the board's structure of standing committees provides the setting in which senior administrators interact with trustees. In the typical board committee system that parallels the institution's administrative structure, vice presidents and others responsible for particular administrative functions usually staff related board committees. Duties include preparing background information and committee agendas, attending committee meetings, and interacting formally and informally with committee members. Trustees, as we have seen, often prefer operational decision making to promulgating broad policy. It would therefore not be surprising if board members found committee work, with its tangible focus on management, more satisfying than board meetings themselves. Moreover, committees usually meet more frequently than the board itself (Taylor 1987). Under such circumstances, the administrator staffing the committee may be more familiar to committee members than the president is (Wood 1984a).

To the extent that trustees grow to depend on staff and value their contributions, the board's estimation of the president's im-

portance may decline (Wood 1984a). At the same time—and
for the same reason—the staff's estimation of the president's
power may be undermined (Middleton 1983). At the extreme,
both trustees and staff members might come to see the president as superfluous.

Presidents interviewed by Wood indicated that they make
special efforts to be involved in committee work: attending
committee meetings, speaking on behalf of staff at executive
committee meetings attended by chairs of standing committees,
and otherwise taking pains to assure trustees that the president
is aware of what each committee is doing and is in control of
the staff and the institution (Wood 1984a).

Suggestions that the president distance the board from staff
as well as faculty and students (Fisher 1984) do not seem practical in light of committees' needs for staff support and the ease
with which trustees and staff may contact each other. And in
any event such a remedy probably misses the point. The committee system that parallels the administrative structure exists to
serve trustees' interest in operational matters. Or, alternatively,
trustees are interested in operational matters because the committee structure has fostered and rewarded that interest. In
either case, the resulting situation is that the board may focus
its attention on administrative matters to the neglect of broad
policy (Wood 1984a). When this situation occurs, the contributions of staff may well take on a higher luster than those of the
president, because that which staff members know and do is
what most interests trustees.

The solution to the dilemma vis-à-vis committees, where it
exists, may include abolishing some standing committees and
shortening the meeting times of those remaining. Ad hoc committees charged with focusing on a given broad topic over a
period of one to three years could then be established. In general, these committees would be concerned with the relationship between the institution and society and might consider
such topics as interinstitutional cooperation and conflict, the effect of student and institutional aid programs on enrollment,
and job opportunities for liberal arts graduates. Ad hoc committees would draw on expertise from many administrative areas
and academic departments (Wood 1985, pp. 148–49).

Two results would likely arise from such an arrangement. No
longer captive to the administrative structure, the board would
begin to consider broad policy issues rather than managerial detail. And the president's stature would be enhanced at the ex-

pense of senior administrators because discussions of an ad hoc committee would draw more on the president's leadership role and vision for the institution than on the specific expertise of a single staff member (Wood 1985, p. 149).

The Board and the Faculty
Sources of the faculty's influence
While the president and by extension senior administrators are delegated considerable authority, primarily as a managerial expedient, faculty are thought to merit a voice in decision making because they are significantly affected by the board's decisions, their competence is essential to the institution's effectiveness, and, as a practical matter and legal authority notwithstanding, it is difficult for any board to govern or any president to lead in the face of significant resistance from faculty (Gould 1973; Kauffman 1980; Keeton 1971).

Fundamentally, the faculty's influence over a board is a function of the legitimation that holders of formal authority require from those who exercise functional authority.

> Leaders . . . try to ensure that whenever they deal with conflict, the decisions reached are widely accepted, not only from a fear of violence, punishment, or coercion, but also from a belief that it is morally right and proper to accept them. Widespread belief in, and commitment to, the rightness of the governing structure, processes, policies, and personnel, and acceptance of this belief, give them "legitimacy." Legitimated influence is highly efficient and effective. It is more reliable and durable than influence dependent on coercion, and it requires a minimum of political resources to be effective. In a complex and changing institution such as a college or university . . . legitimated influence is essential to institutional efficiency and effectiveness (Keeton 1971, pp. 101–2).

Through organized and unrelenting efforts by some faculties, presidents have been forced to resign and structures of governance reformed. In other cases, protesting faculties' failures of tenacity or strategy have left the status quo intact. The point, central to the view of the institution as a political arena, is that the ability to shape the character of an institution is not merely a function of formal authority (Baldridge, Curtis, and Riley 1978; Hartnett 1971).

Particularly during the campus unrest of the 1960s and early 1970s, many faculties called for a greater formal role in institutional decision making, including membership on governing boards (Carnegie Commission 1973a). The movement enjoyed little success, and the number of faculty members serving as trustees of their own or other institutions is miniscule. Nor have faculty senates fared well. Most deal with minor issues, while crucial academic decisions are made at the department level or by administrators (Baldridge, Curtis, and Riley 1978).

Doubtless the same phenomenon described earlier that is responsible for dividing board members into subgroups of activists, spectators, and apathetics (McConnell 1971) operates among faculties, where a small "power elite" works amid a large group who are inactive (Baldridge, Curtis, and Riley 1978). Faculties' narrow interests in matters of governance are also said to contribute to their inactivity. Most are concerned that the governing board understand and appreciate faculty contributions, that the institution obtain more money, and that faculty be insulated from external pressure (Millett 1980b).

In times of institutional crisis, however, differences between trustees and faculty with respect to personal values, division of authority, and the significance of claims by other constituents may erupt into loud and divisive controversy. The infamous mid-20th century controversy over the loyalty oath at the University of California is instructive in this regard. Regents and faculty members battled for years over a regent-imposed requirement for an oath to which faculty objected on grounds of constitutionality and academic freedom.

The issues that divided the regents and the faculties of the University of California then would, both at that institution and at other universities of similar purpose and distinction, tend to govern faculty/trustee relationships today if major differences were once again to divide them. These differences are endemic to the life and character of universities. Both tradition and civility, however, have combined in times of harmony between faculties and governing boards to favor a relationship that has permitted such differences to be quietly understood rather than to be openly expressed. In times of major controversy, however, one or more of these issues nearly always become highly visible and distressing sources of divisiveness between faculties and trustees, thus throwing into relief the fragile and strangely contradictory nature of university life (David Gardner, quoted in Mortimer and Mc-Connell 1978, p. 125).

It is suggested that this and similar crises might have been avoided if regents, administrators, and faculty had conferred regularly on matters of lesser consequence and thus built the mutual trust needed to sustain them in times of greater difficulty (Mortimer and McConnell 1978, pp. 135–36). And, in fact, evidence indicates that morale is higher among faculty groups who feel they have a direct role in institutional governance (Baldridge, Curtis, and Riley 1978), and boards that communicate with faculty are thought to be better informed and more effective than boards that work in isolation (Corson 1973a). For such reasons, many campuses undertake efforts to bring faculty and trustees together informally and in shared arrangements for governance.

Influencing the board

A relatively extensive literature advises trustees of the necessity of sharing authority with faculty members and suggests means of doing so. Emphasized, for example, are the need to divide labor, improve mechanisms for governance, enforce the sharing of authority, increase the efficiency of structures of governance, and develop capable leadership (Keeton 1971, pp. 148–51; see also Carnegie Commission 1973a; Mortimer and Mc-Connell 1978).

Considerably more sparse is the literature advising faculty on means of working more effectively with trustees. Given that trustees are the holders of formal authority, it is perhaps not surprising that with few exceptions the advice given to faculty stresses the importance of good will and cooperation in dealing with trustees and also describes the risks faculty assume in attempting to influence the board through direct contact and participation.

First, faculty are warned that it is unlikely that their colleagues will become involved in sufficient enough numbers that attempts at "participatory democracy" will be truly democratic (Brewster 1971, p. 57). Are the spectators and apathetics willing to have the activists speak for them? Second, just as contacts with administrators encourage many trustees to become involved in managerial detail, some suspect that contact with faculty can lead to the board's interest in the details of teaching and research (Lee and Bowen 1971).

Whether or not they participate directly in board affairs, faculty are offered several suggestions for increasing their influence on institutional governance. First, faculty are advised to support the president (Commission on Strengthening 1984). As has already been argued, the president's position vis-à-vis the board is strengthened by the support of constituents and is undermined by internal squabbling. To the extent that the faculty, working through normal departmental and administrative channels, can come to agreements that the president can support and defend to the board, the faculty's interests are likely to be better served than under arrangements where a few faculty members with direct access to the board presume to speak for their peers. Limited representation of this sort is unlikely to satisfy most faculty, because much of the disagreement between faculty and trustees arises from disagreement over the goals and purposes of the institution itself (Gould 1973). And often the greatest disagreement is found *among* the faculty (Baldridge, Curtis, and Riley 1978).

Second, it is suggested that faculty bear in mind that most boards operate under environmental constraints that limit their range of options. Faculty in public institutions, tuition-dependent independent colleges, or any college or university highly dependent on a single source of income or legitimation cannot always blame their boards when decisions fail to conform to the faculty's opinion. In contrast, in those institutions that are relatively independent of environmental controls, faculties can and usually do substantially influence institutional policy making. But such influence is normally exerted through regular departmental and administrative structures rather than through direct faculty participation in the board's affairs (Baldridge, Curtis, and Riley 1978).

A third suggestion offered to faculty is that they focus on trustees as potential resources rather than as adversaries. Many trustees are knowledgeable, accomplished, well-connected professionals willing to advise and share expertise with faculty and students. The institution that fails to use trustees' personal talents is wasting a valuable asset (Bean 1975).

A fourth and related recommendation offered to the faculty suggests that the trustee who is treated as an ally is likely to be "a more knowledgeable and eloquent defender of the campus in . . . trying times" (Bean 1975, p. 42). At their best, boards have sustained colleges during financial crises, taken principled stands on academic freedom with a sometimes uncomprehending public, and have championed institutions, faculty members, and students under political attack (Gould 1973). Moreover, few faculty would argue that direct government control of colleges and universities—the alternative to lay trusteeship seen in most other nations—is preferable to the American arrangement (Zwingle 1980b).

Faculty unionization

Those who believe that authority for decision making in most institutions rests in the hands of trustees and administrators and that the faculty's authority is largely illusory argue that faculty who want real power must organize and negotiate collectively to obtain it (McConnell 1971). In fact, considerable evidence suggests that efforts to unionize faculty have been more common on poorly managed campuses and those where faculty have had little opportunity to influence policy making (Angell and Kelley 1980; Baldridge, Curtis, and Riley 1978). In this sense, "it has been said that governing boards and administrations probably will get the kind of professional relations and organizations that they deserve" (McConnell 1971, p. 111).

As of 1985, 411 collective bargaining agreements were in force on college and university campuses (Douglas 1986, p. 3). Naturally, such agreements concern matters of compensation and working conditions, but in a few institutions, contracts have been negotiated that delegate *powers* previously held by trustees to committees of faculty and administrators (Angell and Kelley 1980).

In other cases, however, faculty who unionize may actually lose de facto decision-making authority. Nonunionized faculty frequently exert influence on a variety of matters that boards have overlooked out of ignorance or indifference. Once such issues are subjected to negotiation, the faculty's informal authority is likely to decline (Carnegie Commission 1973a). Moreover, administrators working with a unionized faculty "become board agents more clearly than in the preunion past when a benign ambiguity prevailed" (Boyd 1972, p. 269).

While unionization may reduce the informal authority of faculties, it frequently curtails severely the formal authority of administrators and boards in public institutions. Under collective bargaining arrangements, disputes are settled with the individuals who control resources, and in the public sector those individuals are governors and legislators (Carnegie Commission 1973a). In New York State, for example, the State University of New York faculty contract defines the governor—not the board of trustees—as the employer. In this and similar situations, considerable authority for the management of the institution is sacrificed to powerful forces outside the university (Angell and Kelley 1980).

Interestingly, in 1969, 93 percent of a sample of 8,500 faculty members who favored collective bargaining also believed that faculty should be represented on the governing board (Carnegie Commission 1973a). This somewhat inconsistent aspiration—wanting in effect to be both employer and employee—suggests a desire by faculty for influence in any way it can be had rather than a commitment to unionization or board membership per se.

Summary

It is probably more accurate to describe the relationship between trustees and senior administrators, primarily the president, as one of mutual dependence rather than partnership. These "exchange relationships" exchange the board's formal authority for administrators' functional authority. As such, senior administrators can markedly influence a board's work by spending time communicating with trustees, controlling board agendas and background information, influencing the selection and development of trustees, motivating trustees' behavior to the desired ends, establishing strong relationships with faculty and other constituents, and so on.

The relative influence of presidents versus other senior administrators who interact with boards appears to be a function of the nature of the work the board performs. Where standing committees dealing with operational matters predominate, administrators responsible for related functional areas may well establish close relationships with committee members that in some cases may undermine the president's relationship with the board. In contrast, where committees do not exist, where presidents control committee work, or where committees deal with overarching institutional policy rather than day-to-day operations, presidential influence is likely to dominate.

Faculty influence on boards derives from the desire of many administrators and trustees to share authority with faculty and from the fact that influence may result from functional as well as formal authority. Faculty willing to press for a voice in governance are frequently heeded, owing primarily to the political nature of much decision making in colleges and universities.

Faculty members may seek to influence boards in a variety of direct and indirect ways. They are advised first to influence and then support the president and thus strengthen indirectly their own position vis-à-vis the board. Further, faculty should treat trustees as resources and allies, using trustees' talents and strengthening the board's ability to withstand threats from the environment.

Some have suggested that real authority accrues only to faculty who unionize and bargain collectively with their institutions. While this situation may be so in some instances, other unionized faculty have lost informal authority previously held. Moreover, in public institutions, they have sometimes sacrificed institutional authority to external agencies empowered to negotiate and enforce collective bargaining agreements.

SUMMARY AND CONCLUSIONS

Historically, the control of American colleges and universities by lay boards of trustees has been viewed as a means of ensuring simultaneously institutional autonomy and accountability to the public. Theoretically, boards have assumed final responsibility for all institutional decision making, and they have done so as informed but objective outsiders who, unlike administrators and faculty members, are professionally and economically independent of the institution. This position on the boundary of the institution has been thought to enable boards both to interpret the institution to the public and to represent the broad public interest to the institution.

As institutional complexity and professionalization have increased, however, lay boards have become increasingly dependent on the recommendations and independent activities of administrators and faculty members, frequently to such an extent that questions are raised about whether boards of modern institutions can govern at all. At least four facts seem clear:

Boards cannot govern alone, and the functional authority of administrators and faculty members is crucial to legitimating the board's formal authority.

- Boards cannot govern alone, and the functional authority of administrators and faculty members is crucial to legitimating the board's formal authority.
- The formal authority of boards remains a powerful factor in institutional governance, and presidents, in particular, underestimate at their peril both the potential for good or harm that adheres to the board's authority.
- Boards are highly variable among themselves, and individual boards may change over time.
- Boards can be improved, and administrators—especially presidents—and faculty members are powerful determinants of a board's effectiveness.

Boards cannot—and do not—govern alone. Both the prescriptive and descriptive literature on trusteeship emphasizes that boards should and do depend on administrators and faculty members for advice and recommendations. This relationship can be conceived as an exchange relationship in which the formal authority assigned to trustees in institutional charters is exchanged for the functional authority administrators possess by virtue of expertise and full-time commitment to the institution.

The president, in particular, may dominate the board's decision making by controlling the board's agenda and the information boards receive. Trustees may cooperate in this arrangement through their reluctance to spend much time on trusteeship and their inclination to avoid the conflict with the president and with one another that may be associated with more extensive involvement in institutional affairs.

Much of the activity boards undertake is operational rather than concerned with the formulation of broad policy. A system of standing board committees that parallels institutional administrative structures tends to encourage trustees' attention to administrative detail. Moreover, trustees themselves often derive their greatest satisfaction from applying their own professional expertise to the solution of institutional problems, thus serving a consultative rather than a governing role.

The formal authority of boards remains a significant factor in institutional governance. Despite boards' dependence on the professional expertise of administrators and faculty members, trustees remain a potent force on most campuses. They appoint and can dismiss the president. Consequently, the successful president normally gives considerable time and attention to relations with the board and takes pains to inform and involve the board in institutional affairs, if only as a defensive tactic.

In times of scarce resources and institutional stress, the responsibility for making decisions tends to move to higher levels of organizations, and in the case of colleges and universities, it has resulted in greater pressure on governing boards to make decisions that might previously have been ignored or delegated to others. This tendency seems particularly the case among boards governing institutions subject to significant external regulations or pressure; it is often the board that is held accountable by external agencies and groups.

Boards can be an important source of support and legitimation for institutions. Many trustees give and raise money, defend academic norms to a sometimes skeptical public, offer their expertise to the institution, and otherwise enhance the institution's credibility by their willingness to be associated with it. Colleges and universities founded in recent years, both in the United States and England, adopted the model of a lay board for reasons similar to those that historically have justified it: Trustees legitimate the institution and promote its accountability while preventing direct control by government.

Boards are highly variable. Boards vary enormously, attributable to environmental factors, institutional characteristics, and differences in structure, characteristics of individual trustees, and the nature of relations between individual boards and their constituents.

Public boards are frequently subject to intense and specific pressure from appointing agencies and electorates, and considerable controversy surrounds the question of whether the public board's primary loyalty should reside with the institution or the public. So also do pressures from the providers of resources, prospective students, alumni, sponsoring churches, and other forces in the environment affect a board's responsibilities and activities in both public and independent institutions.

Institutional characteristics like size and complexity, faculty and administrative expertise, and financial condition affect the board's work. So also do characteristics of the board— processes of selecting trustees, composition, operating style, committee systems, meeting schedules—help determine the character of the board's activity.

Individual trustees bring particular skills, motivations, and personal characteristics to their boards, which combine to affect the board's character, operating style, and choice of issues with which to become involved. A trustee's profession, proximity to campus, alumni status, and needs for recognition, for example, will influence the board's agenda, the amount of time the trustee spends on campus, and the work he or she does on the board and for the institution.

Boards also vary with respect to the nature of their relationships with constituents. Whether owing to institutional culture, operating style, traditions of faculty authority, personality of the president, institutional size and complexity, or other factors, boards assume differing roles, based in part on the skills and expectations others have of them.

Presidents, other administrators, and faculty members can help make boards more effective. Because boards depend to such a great extent on presidents and other administrators and faculty for information, motivation, education, and selection of new members, institutional personnel can influence the board's activity and effectiveness. Presidents may be tempted to use their control of information and expertise to isolate and mollify their boards. In doing so, however, two sorts of risks are assumed. First, inappropriately informed or unenlightened trustees faced with a crisis may act precipitously or ineffectively to mitigate the problem and may well blame the president who failed to warn them of impending trouble. Second, the president who isolates or ignores the board may sacrifice a valuable opportunity to ensure more effective interaction with the institution's environment. Trustees with ties to sources of external support and legitimation can be motivated to serve as significant resources for institutions in crisis or in transition to higher levels of quality.

Involving the board appropriately in the institution's work requires a significant investment of time and effort by the president and other institutional personnel. It is far easier to involve trustees in operational decision making than in formulation of broad policy. In the short run, trustees' operational activity may seem a safe and productive use of trustees' time. It probably also, however, fails to encourage board members to develop the broad perspective on the institution that is necessary to represent it effectively to its environment and to recognize and respond to threats to the institution's long-term survival and vitality.

REFERENCES

The Educational Resources Information Center (ERIC) Clearinghouse
on Higher Education abstracts and indexes the current literature on
higher education for inclusion in ERIC's data base and announcement
in ERIC's monthly bibliographic journal, *Resources in Education*
(RIE). Most of these publications are available through the ERIC Document Reproduction Service (EDRS). For publications cited in this
bibliography that are available from EDRS, ordering number and price
are included. Readers who wish to order a publication should write to
the ERIC Document Reproduction Service, 3900 Wheeler Avenue, Al-
exandria, Virginia 22304. (Phone orders with VISA or MasterCard are
taken at 800/227-ERIC or 703/823-0500.) When ordering, please spec-
ify the document (ED) number. Documents are available as noted in
microfiche (MF) and paper copy (PC). Because prices are subject to
change, it is advisable to check the latest issue of *Resources in Education* for current cost based on the number of pages in the publication.

Academy for Educational Development. 1985. *Improving Endowment
Management*. Washington, D.C.: Association of Governing Boards
of Universities and Colleges. ED 263 816. 36 pp. MF – $1.00; PC
– $5.44.

Aldrich, Howard E. 1979. *Organizations and Environments*. Engle-
wood Cliffs, N.J.: Prentice-Hall.

Alton, Bruce T. January/February 1982. "Why Presidents Quit."
AGB Reports 24: 47–53.

American Association of University Professors. 1966. "Statement on
Government of Colleges and Universities." *AAUP Bulletin* 52 (4):
375–79.

American Council on Education/Association of Governing Boards of
Universities and Colleges. 1986. *Deciding Who Shall Lead*. Washington, D.C.: Author.

Angell, George W., and Kelley, Edward P., Jr. 1980. "Responding to
Unionism." In *Handbook of College and University Trusteeship*,
edited by Richard T. Ingram and associates. San Francisco: Jossey-
Bass.

Association of American Colleges. 1985. *Integrity in the College Curriculum*. Washington, D.C.: Author.

Association of Governing Boards of Universities and Colleges. Janu-
ary/February 1979. "Guidelines for Policies Affecting Potential
Conflicts of Interest." *AGB Reports* 21: 31–34.

———. 1981. *Illustrative Bylaws for Independent Colleges*. Washington, D.C.: Author. ED 238 372. 22 pp. MF – $1.00; PC – $3.59.

———, Subcommittee on the Role of Trustees in Institutional and
Specialized Accreditation. 1982. *The Board's Role in Accreditation*.
Washington, D.C.: Author. ED 236 975. 20 pp. MF – $1.00; PC –
$3.59.

————. September/October 1985. "Trouble with Your Liability Insurance? Here's Why." *AGB Reports* 27: 24–28.

————. 1986. *Composition of Governing Boards, 1985*. Washington, D.C.: Author. ED 265 810. 45 pp. MF – $1.00; PC – $5.44.

Auerbach, Arnold J. January 1961. "Aspirations of People, Power, and Agency Goals." *Social Work* 6: 66–73.

Bailey, Stephen K. 1982. "Coping with Crises of Funding, Standards, and Purpose: An Expanded Role for Trustees." *Change* 14 (3): 24–29.

Baldridge, J. Victor; Curtis, David V.; and Riley, Gary L. 1978. *Policy Making and Effective Leadership*. San Francisco: Jossey-Bass.

Bean, Atherton. May/June 1975. "The Liberal Arts College Trustee's Next 25 Years." *AGB Reports* 17: 34–43.

Berdahl, Robert O. 1971. *Statewide Coordination of Higher Education*. Washington, D.C.: American Council on Education. ED. pp. MF – $1.00; PC –.

Besse, Ralph M. 1973. "A Comparison of the University with the Corporation." In *The University as an Organization*, edited by James A. Perkins. New York: McGraw-Hill.

Bogue, E. Grady, and Riggs, R.O. 1974. "Institutional Policy and Its Abuses." *Journal of Higher Education* 45 (5): 355–63.

Boyd, William B. May 1972. "The Impact of Collective Bargaining on University Governance." *Liberal Education* 58: 265–71.

Brewster, Kingman. 1971. "Politics of Academia." In *Power and Authority*, edited by Harold L. Hodgkinson and L. Richard Meeth. San Francisco: Jossey-Bass.

Brown, Kathleen M. April 1986. *Applied Empirical Research on Non-profit Organization Management: Survey and Recommendations*. Working Paper No. 1. San Francisco: University of San Francisco, Institute for Nonprofit Organization Management. ED. pp. MF – $1.00; PC –.

Brown, Margaret, and Walworth, William. Winter 1985–86. "Educational Leadership: College Presidents in the Decade Ahead." *The College Board Review* 138: 22–32.

Brubacher, John S., and Rudy, Willis. 1968. *Higher Education in Transition*. New York: Harper & Row.

Carnegie Commission on Higher Education. 1973a. *Governance of Higher Education: Six Priority Problems*. New York: McGraw-Hill.

————. 1973b. *The Purposes and the Performance of Higher Education in the United States: Approaching the Year 2000*. New York: McGraw-Hill.

Carnegie Foundation for the Advancement of Teaching. 1976. *The States and Higher Education*. San Francisco: Jossey-Bass.

————. 1982. *The Control of the Campus*. Washington, D.C.: Author. ED. pp. MF – $1.00; PC –.

Chaffee, Ellen Earle. 1984. *After Decline, What? Survival Strategies at Eight Private Colleges.* Boulder, Colo.: National Center for Higher Education Management Systems. ED 253 131. 140 pp. MF – $1.00; PC – $13.26.

Chait, Richard P. 1984. "The Role and Responsibility of the Academic Affairs Committee." In *Trustee Responsibility for Academic Affairs,* edited by Richard P. Chait. Washington, D.C.: Association of Governing Boards of Universities and Colleges.

Chait, Richard P., and associates. 1984. *Trustee Responsibility for Academic Affairs.* Washington, D.C.: Association of Governing Boards of Universities and Colleges.

Chait, Richard P., and Taylor, Barbara F. 1983. *Academic Affairs Committee.* Washington, D.C.: Association of Governing Boards of Universities and Colleges. ED 238 373. 22 pp. MF – $1.00; PC not available EDRS.

Cheit, Earl F. March 1971. "Regent Watching." *AGB Reports* 13: 4–13.

Clark, Burton R. October 1976. "The Benefits of Disorder." *Change* 8: 31–37.

Cleary, Robert E. November/December 1979. "Who's in Charge Here?" *AGB Reports* 21: 21–26.

———. March/April 1980. "Something Personal about It." *AGB Reports* 22: 39–42.

Cleveland, Harlan. 1985. *The Costs and Benefits of Openness: Sunshine Laws and Higher Education.* Washington, D.C.: Association of Governing Boards of Universities and Colleges. ED 263 814. 66 pp. MF – $1.00; PC – $7.29.

Cohen, Michael D., and March, James G. 1974. *Leadership and Ambiguity: The American College President.* New York: McGraw-Hill.

Columbia University. 1957. *The Role of Trustees of Columbia University.* New York: Author.

———. 1969. *Composition, Structure, and Functioning of the Trustees.* 4th interim report. New York: Columbia University. ED 041 558. 14 pp. MF – $1.00; PC – $3.59.

Commission on Strengthening Presidential Leadership. 1984. *Presidents Make a Difference.* Washington, D.C.: Association of Governing Boards of Universities and Colleges. ED 247 879. 140 pp. MF – $1.00; PC not available EDRS.

Corson, John J. 10 January 1970. "Social Change and the University." *Saturday Review.*

———. July/August 1973a. "The Board of Trustees: Necessity or Anachronism?" *AGB Reports* 15: 4–11.

———. 1973b. "Perspectives on the University Compared with Other Institutions." In *The University as an Organization,* edited by James A. Perkins. New York: McGraw-Hill.

————. 1975. *The Governance of Colleges and Universities*. Rev. ed. New York: McGraw-Hill.

————. January/February 1977. "Trusteeship, 1977 Style." *AGB Reports* 19: 3–5.

————. 1980. "Participating in Policy Making and Management." In *Handbook of College and University Trusteeship*, edited by Richard T. Ingram and associates. San Francisco: Jossey-Bass.

Cote, Lawrence S. January/February 1985. "Presidents and Boards Agree on Leadership Roles." *AGB Reports* 27: 30–32.

Cowley, William H. 1980. *Presidents, Professors, and Trustees*. Edited by Donald T. Williams, Jr. San Francisco: Jossey-Bass.

Cunninggim, Merrimon. 1985. *The Pros and Cons of Advisory Committees*. Washington, D.C.: Association of Governing Boards of Universities and Colleges. ED 263 811. 23 pp. MF – $1.00; PC – $3.59.

Davis, Junius A., and Batchelor, Steve A. 1974. *The Effective College and University Board: A Report of a National Survey of Trustees and Presidents*. Research Triangle Park, N.C.: Research Triangle Institute, Center for Research and Evaluation. ED 100 259. 108 pp. MF – $1.00; PC – $11.41.

Dorsey, Rhoda M. 1980. "Engaging in Institutional Planning." In *Handbook of College and University Trusteeship*, edited by Richard T. Ingram and associates. San Francisco: Jossey-Bass.

Douglas, Joel M., with Kotch, Elizabeth A. 1986. *Directory of Faculty Contracts and Bargaining Agents in Institutions of Higher Education*. New York: Baruch College, City University of New York, National Center for the Study of Collective Bargaining in Higher Education and the Professions. ED 268 919. 249 pp. MF – $1.00; PC not available EDRS.

Duke University. 1970. *The Board of Trustees: Interim Report of the Commission on University Governance*. Durham, N.C.: Author. ED 040 655. 24 pp. MF – $1.00; PC – $3.59.

Duryea, E.D. 1973. "Evolution of University Organization." In *The University as an Organization*, edited by James A. Perkins. New York: McGraw-Hill.

Education Commission of the States. 1986. *State Postsecondary Education Structures Handbook, 1986*. Denver: Author. ED. pp. MF – $1.00; PC –.

Epstein, Leon D. 1974. *Governing the University: The Campus and the Public Interest*. San Francisco: Jossey-Bass.

Fisher, Ben C. 1969. *Duties and Responsibilities of College and University Trustees*. Raleigh, N.C.: North Carolina Board of Higher Education. ED 038 095. 109 pp. MF – $1.00; PC – $11.41.

Fisher, James L. 1984. *The Power of the Presidency*. New York: American Council on Education/Macmillan.

Galbraith, John Kenneth. September 1967. "How the University Can Protect Itself." *College Management* 2: 32–36.

Gale, Robert L. 1984. *Building a More Effective Board*. Washington, D.C.: Association of Governing Boards of Universities and Colleges. ED. pp. MF – $1.00; PC –.

Gilley, J. Wade; Fulmer, Kenneth A.; and Reithlingshoefer, Sally J. 1986. *Searching for Academic Excellence*. New York: American Council on Education/Macmillan.

Gomberg, Irene, and Atelsek, Frank. 1977. *Composition of College and University Governing Boards*. Higher Education Panel Report No. 35. Washington, D.C.: American Council on Education. ED 144 514. 28 pp. MF – $1.00; PC – $3.59.

Gould, Samuel B. 1973. "Trustees and the University Community." In *The University as an Organization*, edited by James A. Perkins. New York: McGraw-Hill.

Greenleaf, Robert K. 1974. *Trustees as Servants*. Cambridge, Mass.: Center for Applied Studies.

Hartnett, Rodney T. 1969. *College and University Trustees: Their Backgrounds and Educational Attitudes*. Princeton, N.J.: Educational Testing Service. ED 028 704. 76 pp. MF – $1.00; PC – $9.56.

———. 1970. *The New College Trustee: Some Predictions for the 1970s*. Princeton, N.J.: Educational Testing Service., ED 045 013. 84 pp. MF – $1.00; PC – $9.56.

———. 1971. "Trustee Power in America." In *Power and Authority*, edited by Harold L: Hodgkinson and L. Richard Meeth. San Francisco: Jossey-Bass.

Hodgkinson, Harold L. May/June 1971. "Some Surprising Thoughts on Tenure, Sanctuary, and Governance." *Change* 3: 15–16.

Hofstadter, Richard, and Metzger, Walter P. 1955. *The Development of Academic Freedom in the United States*. New York: Columbia University Press.

Holderman, James B. 1981. "Trustees Moving to Center Stage." *Educational Record* 62 (1): 34–35.

Ingram, Richard T. 1980a. "Organizing the Board." In *Handbook of College and University Trusteeship*, edited by Richard T. Ingram and associates. San Francisco: Jossey-Bass.

———. 1980b. "Toward Effective Trusteeship for the Eighties." In *Handbook of College and University Trusteeship*, edited by Richard T. Ingram and associates. San Francisco: Jossey-Bass.

———. 1980c. "Trustee Audit." In *Handbook of College and University Trusteeship*, edited by Richard T. Ingram and associates. San Francisco: Jossey-Bass.

———. 1984. *Trustee Orientation and Development Programs*. Washington, D.C.: Association of Governing Boards of Universities and Colleges. ED. pp. MF – $1.00; PC –.

————. 1985. *Executive Committee*. Washington, D.C.: Association of Governing Boards of Universities and Colleges.

Jencks, Christopher, and Riesman, David. 1968. *The Academic Revolution*. Garden City, N.Y.: Doubleday.

Jones, W.T. 1985. "From Guardians to Agents: The Changing Role of Trustees." *Educational Record* 66 (2): 10–15.

Kaiser, Harvey H. 1983. *Buildings and Grounds Committee*. Washington, D.C.: Association of Governing Boards of Universities and Colleges. ED 238 374. 25 pp. MF – $1.00; PC not available EDRS.

————. 1984. *Crumbling Academe*. Washington, D.C.: Association of Governing Boards of Universities and Colleges. ED 247 876. 70 pp. MF – $1.00; PC not available in EDRS.

Kauffman, Joseph F. 1977. "The New College President: Expectations and Realities." *Educational Record* 58 (2): 146–68.

————. 1980. *At the Pleasure of the Board: The Service of the College and University President*. Washington, D.C.: American Council on Education. ED 187 217. 122 pp. MF – $1.00; PC – $11.41.

Keeton, Morris. 1971. *Shared Authority on Campus*. Washington, D.C.: American Association for Higher Education.

Keller, George. 1983. *Academic Strategy: The Management Revolution in American Higher Education*. Baltimore: Johns Hopkins University Press. ED 263 977. 211 pp. MF – $1.00; PC – $21.38.

Kerr, Clark. Winter 1970. "Governance and Functions." *Daedalus*.

Kerr, Clark, and Gade, Marian L. 1986. *The Many Lives of Academic Presidents*. Washington, D.C.: Association of Governing Boards of Universities and Colleges. ED. 267 704. 267 pp. MF – $1.00; PC – $25.50.

Kinnison, William. 1984. *Development Committee*. Washington, D.C.: Association of Governing Boards of Universities and Colleges. ED 263 812. 21 pp. MF – $1.00; PC – $3.59.

Kohn, Patricia F., and Mortimer, Kenneth P. 1983. "Selecting Effective Trustees." *Change* 15 (5): 10–15.

Kramer, Ralph M. October 1965. "Ideology, Status, and Power in Board-Executive Relationships." *Social Work* 10: 107–14.

————. 1981. *Voluntary Agencies in the Welfare State*. Berkeley: University of California Press.

Lascell, David M., and Hallenbeck, Alfred M. 1980. "Contending with Conflicts of Interest and Liability." In *Handbook of College and University Trusteeship*, edited by Richard T. Ingram and associates. San Francisco: Jossey-Bass.

Lavine, John M. January/February 1980. "The Value of a Single System." *AGB Reports* 22: 31–34.

Lee, Eugene C., and Bowen, Frank M. 1971. *The Multicampus University: A Study of Academic Governance*. New York: McGraw-Hill.

―――. 1975. *Managing Multicampus Systems: Effective Administration in an Unsteady State*. San Francisco: Jossey-Bass.

Lewis, Robert C. 1980. "Building Effective Trustee Leadership, or How to Exploit Your Trustees." *Educational Record* 61 (4): 18–31.

McConnell, T.R. 1971. "Faculty Government." In *Power and Authority*, edited by Harold L. Hodgkinson and L. Richard Meeth. San Francisco: Jossey-Bass.

McGrath, Earl. 1971. "Who Should Have the Power?" In *Power and Authority*, edited by Harold L. Hodgkinson and L. Richard Meeth. San Francisco: Jossey-Bass.

Mahoney, Brooke W., ed. 1985. *The Role of the Board Chairman or President*. New York: Volunteer Consulting Group.

Manne, Henry G. October 1972. "The Political Economy of Modern Universities." *AGB Reports* 15: 2–13.

Martin, Harold L. 1974. "The Board of Trustees and the Making of Academic Policy." Speech presented at the 10th Annual Conference on the Leadership Role of the Trustee, March 5, New York, New York. ED 093 220. 4 pp. MF – $1.00; PC – $3.59.

Mason, Henry L. 1972. "College and University Government." *Tulane Studies in Political Science* 14.

Meardy, William H. 1977. "Working Relationship between Presidents and Trustees." *Proceedings of the Annual Governor's Workshop for Community College Trustees*. Tallahassee: Florida State Department of Education. ED. pp. MF – $1.00; PC –.

Meeth, L. Richard. 1971. "Administration and Leadership." In *Power and Authority*, edited by Harold L. Hodgkinson and L. Richard Meeth. San Francisco: Jossey-Bass.

Meyerson, Martin. 1980. "Overseeing Academic Programs." In *Handbook of College and University Trusteeship*, edited by Richard T. Ingram and associates. San Francisco: Jossey-Bass.

Middleton, Melissa. 1983. *The Place and Power of Nonprofit Boards of Directors*. New Haven, Conn.: Yale University, Institution for Social and Policy Studies, Program on Nonprofit Organizations. ED. pp. MF – $1.00; PC –.

Millett, John D. 1980a. "Relating Governance to Leadership." In *Improving Academic Management: A Handbook of Planning and Institutional Research*, edited by Paul Jedamus and Marvin Peterson. San Francisco: Jossey-Bass.

―――. 1980b. "Working with Faculty and Students." In *Handbook of College and University Trusteeship*, edited by Richard T. Ingram and associates. San Francisco: Jossey-Bass.

―――. 1984. *Conflict in Higher Education. State Government Coordination versus Institutional Independence*. San Francisco: Jossey-Bass.

Morison, Samuel Eliot. 1935. *The Founding of Harvard College*. Cambridge, Mass.: Harvard University Press.

Mortimer, Kenneth P., and McConnell, T.R. 1978. *Sharing Authority Effectively*. San Francisco: Jossey-Bass.

Munitz, Barry. 1980. "Reviewing Presidential Leadership." In *Handbook of College and University Trusteeship*, edited by Richard T. Ingram and associates. San Francisco: Jossey-Bass.

———. September/October 1981. "Memo to a Multicampus Trustee . . . From a Flagship CEO." *AGB Reports* 23: 19–25.

Nason, John W. 1982. *The Nature of Trusteeship*. Washington, D.C.: Association of Governing Boards of Universities and Colleges. ED 226 648. 127 pp. MF – $1.00; PC not available EDRS.

———. 1984. *Presidential Assessment*. Washington, D.C.: Association of Governing Boards of Universities and Colleges. ED. pp. MF – $1.00; PC –.

———. 1985. *Trustee Responsibilities*. Washington, D.C.: Association of Governing Boards of Universities and Colleges. ED. pp. MF – $1.00; PC –.

National Commission on College and University Trustee Selection. 1980a. *Recommendations for Improving Trustee Selection in Private Colleges and Universities*. Washington, D.C.: Association of Governing Boards of Universities and Colleges. ED 194 028. 48 pp. MF – $1.00; PC – $5.44.

———. 1980b. *Recommendations for Improving Trustee Selection in Public Colleges and Universities*. Washington, D.C.: Association of Governing Boards of Universities and Colleges. ED 194 029. 56 pp. MF – $1.00; PC – $7.29.

Nelson, Charles A. July/August 1973. "Trustees: Serve or Resign." *AGB Reports* 15: 12–21.

———. September/October 1979. "Improving Your Meetings Four Ways." *AGB Reports* 21: 26–29.

———. 1980. "Managing Resources." In *Handbook of College and University Trusteeship*, edited by Richard T. Ingram and associates. San Francisco: Jossey-Bass.

———. 1982. *Trustees and Resource Management*. Washington, D.C.: Association of Governing Boards of Universities and Colleges. ED 196 359. 9 pp. MF – $1.00; PC – $3.59.

———. 1985. *Policy versus Administration*. Washington, D.C.: Association of Governing Boards of Universities and Colleges. ED 262 674. 12 pp. MF – $1.00; PC – $3.59.

Newman, Frank. October 1973. "Trustee Accountability and National Policy." *AGB Reports* 16: 2–8.

———. 10 July 1986. *Public Policy and Political Intrusion in the University* (draft). Denver: Education Commission of the States.

O'Connell, Brian. 1985. *The Board Member's Book*. New York: Foundation Center.

Odendahl, Teresa, and Boris, Elizabeth. May/June 1983. "A Delicate

Balance: Foundation-Board Staff Relations." *Foundation News:* 34–45.

Paltridge, James G. March 1974. "Folklore and Some Facts about Trustee Decisions." *AGB Reports* 16: 20–27.

———. 1980. "Studying Board Effectiveness." In *Handbook of College and University Trusteeship,* edited by Richard T. Ingram and associates. San Francisco: Jossey-Bass.

Paltridge, James G.; Hurst, Julie; and Morgan, Anthony. 1973. *Boards of Trustees: Their Decision Patterns.* Berkeley: University of California–Berkeley, Center for Research and Development in Higher Education. ED 085 035. 103 pp. MF – $1.00; PC – $11.41.

Parsons, Talcott. 1947. "Introduction." In *The Theory of Social and Economic Organization,* by Max Weber. New York: Free Press.

Perkins, James A. 1973. "Conflicting Responsibilities of Governing Boards." In *The University as an Organization,* edited by James A. Perkins. New York: McGraw-Hill.

Pettit, Lawrence K. 1987. "The Administration of Public University Systems: An Organizing Perspective." In *When Colleges Lobby States,* edited by Leonard E. Goodall. Washington, D.C.: American Association of State Colleges and Universities.

Pfeffer, Jeffrey. 1973. "Size, Composition, and Function of Hospital Board Directors: A Study of Organization-Environment Linkage." *Administrative Science Quarterly* 18: 349–64.

Pfeffer, Jeffrey, and Salancik, Gerald R. 1978. *The External Control of Organizations: A Resource Dependence Perspective.* New York: Harper & Row.

Pocock, John W. 1980. "Reporting Finances." In *Handbook of College and University Trusteeship,* edited by Richard T. Ingram and associates. San Francisco: Jossey-Bass.

———. 1984a. *The Board Chairperson and the President.* Washington, D.C.: Association of Governing Boards of Universities and Colleges. ED. pp. MF – $1.00; PC –.

———. 1984b. *Finance Committee.* Washington, D.C.: Association of Governing Boards of Universities and Colleges. ED 238 375. 20 pp. MF – $1.00; PC not available in EDRS.

Pray, Francis C. 1974. *The State of the Art of College Trusteeship: A Situation Review.* Arlington, Va.: Frantzreb & Pray Associates.

———. 1975. *A New Look at Community College Boards of Trustees and Their Relationships: Suggestions for Change.* Washington, D.C.: American Association of Community and Junior Colleges. ED 105 951. 43 pp. MF – $1.00; PC – $5.44.

Price, James L. December 1963. "The Impact of Governing Boards on Organizational Effectiveness and Morale." *Administrative Science Quarterly* 8: 361–77.

Radock, Michael. 1983. *The Fund-Raising Role.* Washington, D.C.:

Association of Governing Boards of Universities and Colleges. ED 196 354. 7 pp. MF – $1.00; PC – $3.59.

Radock, Michael, and Jacobson, Harvey K. 1980. "Securing Resources." In *Handbook of College and University Trusteeship,* edited by Richard T. Ingram and associates. San Francisco: Jossey-Bass.

Rauh, Morton A. 1969. *The Trusteeship of Colleges and Universities.* New York: McGraw-Hill.

———. 1973. "Internal Organization of the Board." In *The University as an Organization,* edited by James A. Perkins. New York: McGraw-Hill.

Rudolph, Frederick. 1962. *The American College and University: A History.* New York: Knopf.

Ruml, Beardsley, and Morrison, Donald H. 1959. *Memo to a College Trustee.* New York: McGraw-Hill.

Savage, Thomas J. 1982. *The Cheswick Process: Seven Steps to a More Effective Board.* Boston: Cheswick Center.

Scarlett, Mel. September/October 1980. "Why Presidents Don't Like State Boards." *AGB Reports* 22: 23-26.

Schenkel, Walter. 1971. "Who Has Been in Power?" In *Power and Authority,* edited by Harold L. Hodgkinson and L. Richard Meeth. San Francisco: Jossey-Bass.

Senor, James. April 1963. "Another Look at the Board-Executive Relationship." *Social Work* 8: 19–25.

Stroup, Herbert. 1966. *Bureaucracy in Higher Education.* New York: Free Press.

Sweet, David E. January/February 1980. "What's Wrong with State Boards." *AGB Reports* 22: 29–30.

Taylor, Barbara E. 1984a. "Academic Budgets." In *Trustee Responsibility for Academic Affairs,* edited by Richard P. Chait. Washington, D.C.: Association of Governing Boards of Universities and Colleges.

———. 1984b. *Trustee Responsibility for Academic Affairs: Results of a National Survey.* Washington, D.C.: Association of Governing Boards of Universities and Colleges.

———. 1987. *Results of a National Survey of Governing Board Characteristics, Policies, and Practices.* Washington, D.C.: Association of Governing Boards of Universities and Colleges.

Trow, Martin A. 1984. *The University Presidency: Comparative Reflections on Leadership.* Urbana, Ill.; University of Illinois.

Veysey, Laurence R. 1965. *The Emergence of the American University.* Chicago: University of Chicago Press.

Weeks, Kent M. 1980. *Trustees and Preventive Law.* Washington, D.C.: Association of Governing Boards of Universities and Colleges. ED 196 357. 10 pp. MF – $1.00; PC – $3.59.

Wessell, Nils Y. January 1974. "Board-President Relationships: Second Thoughts." *AGB Reports* 16: 3–15.

Whitehead, John C. 1985. Remarks in *The Role of the Board Chairman or President,* edited by Brooke W. Mahoney. New York: Volunteer Consulting Group.

Wood, Miriam Mason. 1984a. "Crosscurrents and Undercurrents in the Trustee-President Relationship." *Educational Record* 65 (1): 38–43.

———. 1984b. "Guidelines for an Academic Affairs Committee." In *Trustee Responsibility for Academic Affairs,* edited by Richard P. Chait. Washington, D.C.: Association of Governing Boards of Universities and Colleges.

———. 1985. *Trusteeship in the Private College.* Baltimore: Johns Hopkins University Press.

Woodruff, Bruce E. November/December 1976. "Trustees Must Know the Law." *AGB Reports* 18: 11–18.

Zald, Mayer N. November 1967. "Urban Differentiation, Characteristics of Boards of Directors, and Organizational Effectiveness." *American Journal of Sociology* 73: 261–72.

———. July 1969. "The Power and Functions of Boards of Directors: A Theoretical Synthesis." *American Journal of Sociology* 75: 97–111.

Zwingle, J.L. 1980a. "Assessing Institutional Performance." In *Handbook of College and University Trusteeship,* edited by Richard T. Ingram and associates. San Francisco: Jossey-Bass.

———. 1980b. "Evolution of Lay Governing Boards." In *Handbook of College and University Trusteeship,* edited by Richard T. Ingram and associates. San Francisco: Jossey-Bass.

———. July/August 1981. "Conflict in the Boardroom." *AGB Reports* 23: 28–32.

———. 1985. *Effective Trusteeship.* 3d rev. ed. Washington, D.C.: Association of Governing Boards of Universities and Colleges. ED. pp. MF – $1.00; PC –.

Zwingle, J.L., and Mayville, William V. 1974. *College Trustees: A Question of Legitimacy.* ERIC-AAHE Higher Education Report No. 10. Washington, D.C.: American Association for Higher Education. ED 101 619. 60 pp. MF – $1.00; PC – $7.29.

INDEX

A

AAUP (see American Association of University Professors)
Academic decision-making, 28, 30–31, 38, 50, 72–73
Academic freedom, 6, 93, 95
ACE (see American Council on Education)
Accountability, 64, 65, 67
Accreditation, 33–34
"Activists" vs. "spectators," 78
Ad hoc committees, 31, 40, 60
Administrative policy/responsibility, 37
Administrator relationship with board, 90–92, 101
Advisory boards, 63
AGB (see Association of Governing Boards of Universities and
   Colleges)
Age of trustees, 11, 17
Agenda
       material covered, 61
       planning, 62, 67, 75–76
Alumni as trustees, 4, 15, 39
American Association of University Professors (AAUP), 6, 69
American Council on Education (ACE), 69
Arbitration of disputes, 32–33
Assessment of board, 64–67
Association of Governing Boards of Universities and Colleges (AGB),
   67, 69
Authority (see also Delegation of authority; Shared authority), 9–10,
   25, 44–45, 51–52, 69, 92, 100

B

Balance of power, 78–79
Blacks, 17
Board chair/president relationship, 89–90
Board/faculty relationship, 92–97, 101
Board/president relationship, 71–89, 99–101
Board/senior administrators relationship, 90–92, 101
Budget approval, 28–29
Buffer role, 34
Bureaucratic governance model, 42
Business people as trustees, 4, 5, 11
Butler, Nicholas Murray, 6

C

Cambridge model, 3, 7
Campus facilities maintenance, 29
Chairmanship, 26, 53–55, 58, 89–90
Change agent role, 34

Two-year institutions, 17, 47, 50

U
Unionization, 96–97
University of California, 93

V
Values: changing, 45–46
Vice chair of board, 53
Vice presidents, 90

W
William and Mary, College of, 3
Women as trustees, 11, 13, 17
Working decisions, 40
Workshops on trusteeship, 80

Y
Yale University, 3, 4

ASHE-ERIC HIGHER EDUCATION REPORTS

Since 1983, the Association for the Study of Higher Education (ASHE) and the ERIC Clearinghouse on Higher Education at The George Washington University have cosponsored the ASHE-ERIC Higher Education Report series. The 1987 series is the sixteenth overall, with the American Association for Higher Education having served as cosponsor before 1983.

Each monograph is the definitive analysis of a tough higher education problem, based on a thorough research of pertinent literature and institutional experiences. After topics are identified by a national survey, noted practitioners and scholars write the reports, with experts reviewing each manuscript before publication.

Eight monographs (10 monographs before 1985) in the ASHE-ERIC Higher Education Report series are published each year, available individually or by subscription. Subscription to eight issues is $60 regular; $50 for members of AERA, AAHE, and AIR; $40 for members of ASHE (add $7.50 for postage outside the United States).

Prices for single copies, including 4th class postage and handling, are $10.00 regular and $7.50 for members of AERA, AAHE, AIR, and ASHE ($7.50 regular and $6.00 for members for 1983 and 1984 reports, $6.50 regular and $5.00 for members for reports published before 1983). If faster 1st class postage is desired for U.S. and Canadian orders, add $.75 for each publication ordered; overseas, add $4.50. For VISA and MasterCard payments, include card number, expiration date, and signature. Orders under $25 must be prepaid. Bulk discounts are available on orders of 15 or more reports (not applicable to subscriptions). Order from the Publications Department, ASHE-ERIC Higher Education Reports, The George Washington University, One Dupont Circle, Suite 630, Washington, D.C. 20036-1183, or phone us at 202/296-2597. Write for a publication list of all the Higher Education Reports available.

1987 ASHE-ERIC Higher Education Reports

1. Incentive Early Retirement Programs for Faculty: Innovative Responses to a Changing Environment
   Jay L. Chronister and Thomas R. Kepple, Jr.

2. Working Effectively with Trustees: Building Cooperative Campus Leadership
   Barbara E. Taylor

1986 ASHE-ERIC Higher Education Reports

1. Post-tenure Faculty Evaluation: Threat or Opportunity?
   Christine M. Licata

2. Blue Ribbon Commissions and Higher Education: Changing Academe from the Outside
   Janet R. Johnson and Laurence R. Marcus

3. Responsive Professional Education: Balancing Outcomes and Opportunities
   Joan S. Stark, Malcolm A. Lowther, and Bonnie M.K. Hagerty

4. Increasing Students' Learning: A Faculty Guide to Reducing Stress among Students
   Neal A. Whitman, David C. Spendlove, and Claire H. Clark

5. Student Financial Aid and Women: Equity Dilemma?
   Mary Moran

---

6. The Master's Degree: Tradition, Diversity, Innovation
   Judith S. Glazer

7. The College, the Constitution, and the Consumer Student: Implications for Policy and Practice
   Robert M. Hendrickson and Annette Gibbs

8. Selecting College and University Personnel: The Quest and the Questions
   Richard A. Kaplowitz

1985 ASHE-ERIC Higher Education Reports

1. Flexibility in Academic Staffing: Effective Policies and Practices
   Kenneth P. Mortimer, Marque Bagshaw, and Andrew T. Masland

2. Associations in Action: The Washington, D.C., Higher Education Community
   Harland G. Bloland

3. And on the Seventh Day: Faculty Consulting and Supplemental Income
   Carol M. Boyer and Darrell R. Lewis

4. Faculty Research Performance: Lessons from the Sciences and Social Sciences
   John W. Creswell

5. Academic Program Reviews: Institutional Approaches, Expectations, and Controversies
   Clifton F. Conrad and Richard F. Wilson

6. Students in Urban Settings: Achieving the Baccalaureate Degree
   Richard C. Richardson, Jr., and Louis W. Bender

7. Serving More Than Students: A Critical Need for College Student Personnel Services
   Peter H. Garland

8. Faculty Participation in Decision Making: Necessity or Luxury?
   Carol E. Floyd

1984 ASHE-ERIC Higher Education Reports

1. Adult Learning: State Policies and Institutional Practices
   K. Patricia Cross and Anne-Marie McCartan

2. Student Stress: Effects and Solutions
   Neal A. Whitman, David C. Spendlove, and Claire H. Clark

3. Part-time Faculty: Higher Education at a Crossroads
   Judith M. Gappa

4. Sex Discrimination Law in Higher Education: The Lessons of the Past Decade
   J. Ralph Lindgren, Patti T. Ota, Perry A. Zirkel, and Nan Van Gieson

5. Faculty Freedoms and Institutional Accountability: Interactions and Conflicts
   Steven G. Olswang and Barbara A. Lee

6. The High-Technology Connection: Academic/Industrial Cooperation for Economic Growth
   Lynn G. Johnson

7. Employee Educational Programs: Implications for Industry and Higher Education
   Suzanne W. Morse

8. Academic Libraries: The Changing Knowledge Centers of Colleges and Universities
   Barbara B. Moran

9. Futures Research and the Strategic Planning Process: Implications for Higher Education
   James L. Morrison, William L. Renfro, and Wayne I. Boucher

10. Faculty Workload: Research, Theory, and Interpretation
    Harold E. Yuker

1983 ASHE-ERIC Higher Education Reports

1. The Path to Excellence: Quality Assurance in Higher Education
   Laurence R. Marcus, Anita O. Leone, and Edward D. Goldberg

2. Faculty Recruitment, Retention, and Fair Employment: Obligations and Opportunities
   John S. Waggaman

3. Meeting the Challenges: Developing Faculty Careers
   Michael C.T. Brookes and Katherine L. German

4. Raising Academic Standards: A Guide to Learning Improvement
   Ruth Talbott Keimig

5. Serving Learners at a Distance: A Guide to Program Practices
   Charles E. Feasley

6. Competence, Admissions, and Articulation: Returning to the Basics in Higher Education
   Jean L. Preer

7. Public Service in Higher Education: Practices and Priorities
   Patricia H. Crosson

8. Academic Employment and Retrenchment: Judicial Review and Administrative Action
   Robert M. Hendrickson and Barbara A. Lee

9. Burnout: The New Academic Disease
   Winifred Albizu Meléndez and Rafael M. de Guzmán

10. Academic Workplace: New Demands, Heightened Tensions
    Ann E. Austin and Zelda F. Gamson

NOTES

NOTES

NOTES